## GINGER M. SULLIVAN
INDIVIDUAL, COUPLE & GROUP PSYCHOTHERAPY

Congratulations on winning the Book Giveaway!

If you enjoy *The Road Out*, please ...

Tell all your friends,

And

Write a kind review on Amazon.com, Goodreads and Barnes and Noble.com.

I would very much appreciate it!

For the rise of your life ...

Ginger M. Sullivan, MA, LPC, CGP
3000 Connecticut Avenue, NW · Suite 210 · Washington, DC 20008
Phone: (202) 265-5855 | Email: vmsmail@aol.com | www.gingersullivan.org

★ - 1 star - Awful

# The Road Out:
## Musings from a Southern Wanderlust

### Ginger M. Sullivan

© 2018 Ginger M. Sullivan

All Rights Reserved.

No part of this publication may be reproduced, stored in a retrieval system, or transmitted, in any form or by any means, electronic, mechanical, photocopying, recording, or otherwise, without the written permission of the author.

First published by Dog Ear Publishing
4011 Vincennes Rd
Indianapolis, IN 46268
www.dogearpublishing.net

ISBN: 978-1-4575-6199-3

This book is printed on acid-free paper.

Printed in the United States of America

For my father

Chapter 1 was the only good part.... down hill after that

Chapter 1 was
The only good
part.... doesn't
kill after that

# Table of Contents

Preface ........................................................................... vii
Introduction ....................................................................... 1

1. On Being A Fatherless Daughter ........................................ 3
2. Step by Step ............................................................... 8
3. Scripted ................................................................... 13
4. Colorless Love ........................................................... 18
5. Show Me the Food ..................................................... 26
6. First Day of School .................................................... 30
7. Drop-Off Magic ......................................................... 34
8. Crazy Love ............................................................... 37
9. Happily, Ever After .................................................... 41
10. The Magic Kingdom .................................................. 45
11. No Stopping Now ..................................................... 49
12. My Shabby Chic Dresser ............................................. 53
13. Kick His A** ........................................................... 57
14. Pulling Teeth ........................................................... 63
15. The Center Hill Hyatt ................................................ 67
16. Loving the Life You Have ........................................... 72
    Acknowledgements ................................................... 76
    Disclaimer .............................................................. 78

*[Handwritten note: for such a small book it packs a lot of nonsense!]*

Small book for such a
packs a lot of
konsonist?

# *Preface*

I started writing accidently, in bursts and spurts. I'd be driving, standing in the shower, or lying in bed, and the urge to write, to record my thoughts, ideas, and emotions, would take hold of me and not let me go until I relented. When words poured out of me like water from an open fire hose, I would panic, snatch a random envelope, and grab my sentiments, trying to save them before they capsized under the next thought that came crashing behind it. My insides were erupting, and writing became my refuge.

At some point, I shared my conglomeration of words—this prosaic pus—with some innocent, yet willing, readers. They responded positively and told me to keep writing, saying that my prose style was "conversational" and "practically deep." I wasn't clear what that meant, but it encouraged me enough to continue.

Wielding the written word is a different skill set from the one I use daily as a psychotherapist, and I enjoyed the change. I primarily listen to other people's words, absorb their deepest reflections and emotions, and help them find meaning in the connection. Like the Great Oz, I pose behind a curtain of detachment, blocking out my own thoughts and feelings—occasionally even from myself.

But writing personal essays demands the opposite posture. It dares the writer to draw from their own life, constructing graphs and charts to illustrate something larger, some truth that can resonate with others. By opening that green velvet curtain, I expose my soul as a fellow human being. I reveal that the landscape beyond my drape is not all sunshine and roses. It contains switchbacks, potholes, and detours. It comprises exhaustion and hope, gain and loss, opportunities and threats. It is ugly and messy while also being imperfectly beautiful.

My fantasy is that, like the psychotherapy I practice within the walls of my office, these essays will affect you and change you for the better. May they rattle your insides, dislodge you from your comfort zone, and propel you toward the best you possible. If that happens, I have done my job.

# *Introduction*

My psychoanalyst, a Jewish man from New York, has never lived anywhere close to the South. After hearing some of the more telling tales of my upbringing in Tennessee, he jokingly encapsulates the essence of my childhood as "having been raised in a trailer park." We both laugh at his simultaneously real, yet also rather exaggerated, depiction. While rich in dollars by almost anyone's measure, my family led a simple existence. We were grounded with grit and determination, homegrown, and emotionally straightforward—at least at eye-level.

I left that home for a world I was neither nurtured for nor naturally attuned to survive, clearing my own path through alien brush, paddling upstream in a canoe for one. My missives home made no sense to my kin. My thoughts, feelings, inclinations, and choices were unrecognizable to and unsupported by those in my bloodline. To them, I had gone astray and become a "Northern radical feminist."

These essays enact a return to my roots. They are stories from my woods, snippets of my struggles, depictions of my character's formation. Like characters in fiction, we all have our backstories. These are mine.

"The shell must break before the bird can fly…"
- Tennyson

"You have to keep breaking your heart until it opens."
- Rumi

"Those who do not move, do not notice their chains."
- Rosa Luxemburg

# 1
## On Being a Fatherless Daughter

The last time I saw my father was Labor Day weekend of 1987. Our family had gathered in Memphis for my younger brother's first college football game, and I had driven eight hours north from southern Mississippi, where I had just begun graduate studies in clinical psychology. Only recently stranded in the friendless desert of the Deep South, I had been looking forward to a weekend of familiarity. If nothing else, I wouldn't be alone in my apartment, microwaving Lean Cuisines and watching mindless reruns of Cheers.

Before my white Toyota Tercel had even come to a complete stop in my uncle's driveway, my short, balding, effervescent father had run out the front door to greet me. He leapt at me—much like a dog upon the homecoming of its master—in an outpouring of enthusiasm and love. I was back on recognizable turf, in the arms of the first man I had ever loved.

Three weeks later, he was dead.

It now seems like a lifetime ago: the time when I had a father. He died before seeing fifty. I was still perched on that uncomfortable boundary between know-it-all teenager and frightened, paralyzed young adult, looking out on an unknown horizon I was unprepared for. His window of opportunity to cement a permanent impression on my burgeoning adult-self had been cut short.

Sometimes I wonder if it wasn't an accident. He had established my brothers and me on the next course in our lives, completed that initial launch into adulthood, and then, poof, he was gone. He exited life, like he was clocking out of a job. My older brother had just gotten married three weeks earlier. My younger brother had just left home for college. And I had started graduate school in my field of choice. He had just settled me into my first apartment, complete with homemade bookshelves and furniture he had painted with his own hands. We three kids had begun our independent lives. Perhaps he decided that we did not need him anymore, that his responsibility was met. He was the stake that supported us as we grew from the ground up toward the sun. Once we could stand on our own, the stake vanished.

A few weeks before he died, I had a slobbery, hair-pulling meltdown. Our family was celebrating a milestone event: my older brother's wedding. I was the only female to join in the traditional male fun of pulling a prank at the ceremony, and as a result, a middle-aged female attendee—a woman well beyond her own having-fun years—verbally assaulted me. She aggressively shamed my behavior, telling me it was inappropriate to join in such tomfoolery. She had no such similar words for my male kin.

My young self was devastated. I did not yet have the internal defenses to let her verbal attack slide off my heart. Instead of getting mad and making it about her—as I would have done in later years, after gaining more maturity and self-assurance—I spiraled down a path of distressed mortification. I needed a life vest, someone to pull me out of my quicksand of shame. And I realized whom I wanted and needed to be that lifesaver: my father. I knew I could count on him to ground me and talk me out of the dark hole my humiliated soul wanted to crawl into. And he did. We sat in my hotel room for hours, talking, while the rest of the partygoers whooped it up at the bar. He told me how proud he was that I had chosen a profession of my own—a profession of meaning and significance—rather than simply following the well-worn family path of dentistry. He believed I was pointed in the right direction to be successful in my life.

Then, a month later, he was gone. Forever.

He went out on opening day of deer season, as he always did. My father liked to hunt with a bow, which meant he would wear camouflage, sit in a three-by-four-foot tree stand several yards above the ground, and wait for deer to wander by below. My father always set his stand rather high, so he could get a better view; this day was no different. When he failed to show up at the designated rendezvous, his hunting partner went searching for him. He found my father lying on the ground, his body already cold. He had evidently fallen from his high perch. All attempts to revive him were for naught. It was too late; he was gone.

There was no warning, no goodbye.

I received one of those emergency phone calls from my dad's best friend. He told me that my dad had been in an accident, and I immediately conjured a hospital scene I would rush home to. I pictured a crowded hospital room where my family would–with our usual sarcasm and humor–coax my father back to health. I couldn't even contemplate the possibility I would henceforth have to move through life without him. My tolerable, possibly even heartwarming, fantasy shattered as my dad's friend continued: "He didn't make it."

Getting out of Hattiesburg, Mississippi, was its own adventure. Not wanting me to drive the many miles north solo, my family sent my dad's brother, his pilot friend, and a four-seater plane to bring me home for the funeral. Once we were securely buckled in, no one said a word for the entire flight. There was nothing to say.

Upon entering my childhood home, I was struck by the standing-room-only scene. The crowd silenced their small talk and stared at me, as if I were a rock star who had shown up late to her own show. I turned a blind eye to them and their Southern casseroles as I wove through their in-the-way bodies. I recognized that they meant well, that they wanted to help. But what could they do? I made a beeline for the master bedroom, where the inner circle stood, still too dumbfounded to even grieve. They too did not know what to say or do with this new horrific normal.

Somehow, we rallied. My mother, brothers, and I mustered whatever we needed to to bury my still-young father. To clear out his belongings. To move my mother from our childhood home to a more appropriately sized apartment. To build our adult lives without his presence, his strength, his contagious energy, his love, and his advice. To live without his high expectations, his undaunted work ethic, and his stern pressure to always achieve in all things.

The remaining four of us had no choice but to negotiate with this new reality in which the center of our family had been surgically removed. Like a paper doll snipped from the middle of the chain, we were left untethered, marooned, forced to make do with a gaping hole in our midst. You never know what rabbit you can pull from your hat until you must. You stick your hand in and yank the damn hare out. By sheer force, we all do what we must to keep the show going.

So here I am: a grown woman. I've spent more time living without my father than with him. Not only do I still miss him, I often wonder what my life would have been like if he had been around longer. Would I have launched into the adult world more securely? Would I have made fewer mistakes? Would I have saved more money and made better financial decisions thanks to his advice? Would he have warned me not to marry *that* one? Would he delight in my children's presence as much as I do? And then there is the other side of these questions. Life always has another side. Without such a significant loss so early in my life, how different of a person would I be today? Would I be spoiled, entitled, and superficial? Would I be less understanding? Would I have less space within myself to hold the pain of others? Would I be less aware that life can change in a flash, that it can alter with a phone call? I will never know the answers to these questions.

I recall one poignant and humorous conversation we had toward the end of his life, when I was a young college student and budding woman. We were hanging out on his turf, in his favorite man cave: the musty garage. I told him subtly, with much intended gratitude in my voice, "Dad, you know you raised me to be a feminist, don't you?"

You would have thought I told him I had joined a cult. "I did not!" He immediately and vehemently denied my claim. My good ole' boy Southern father did not know how to spell, pronounce, or use the word "feminist" properly.

But, just as he taught me, I stood my ground. "It's too late," I told him. "The job has been done." I explained that he had raised me to believe in myself, to set goals and then work to achieve them, to develop determination, to use all my gifts and talents, and to never let my gender stand in the way.

"Oh," he said, looking down in shame after I had finished my explanation, "I guess I did do that."

I often catch myself channeling his energy, refusing to let his vitality dissipate. Because he existed, I do, too. His energy and spirit mattered. His life mattered, and I refuse to let it stop mattering. Just as my dad used to stand beside the track yelling, "Go, Ginge!" as I turned the curve, I also became the obnoxious parental cheerleader. I win the soccer-mom contest for volume. While the other moms chat about all-things-motherly, I stand next to the overly involved dads who are watching the game.

During one game last season, some two-ton Tessie on the opponent's team flagrantly shoved my daughter to the ground. Not even waiting to see if my daughter was okay, I reactively screamed across the field, "Push her back!" The more proper soccer moms—who suddenly paid attention—chided me. "I should be more demure," I scolded myself, tapping into that ever-ready supply of shame. It's probably never gonna happen. For some, legacies cannot—will not, should not—ever die.

Good or bad, we are what we experience. We absorb what we live. We carry on what we have known. That's how legacy works. Unless we actively and intentionally alter that legacy, as I have so often done with much of my history. But in this instance, I will claim my history. I am the loud one on the soccer game's sidelines, the never-meant-to-be feminist, the oft-stupid risk-taker. I am my father's daughter.

# 2
# *Step by Step*

It's hard to believe almost forty years have passed. I was a spry young thing back then, all of fourteen, a mysterious, unknown underdog. Loved ones worried whether I ate enough, my rail-thinness noticeable despite my baggy clothes. People wondered why on earth I always woke at seven a.m. on weekend mornings and was quickly dressed and out the door, regardless of the weather.

One time, my girlfriends kidnapped several of us for a surprise breakfast on an early Saturday morning. Their idea was to drag everyone out of bed so we could have pancakes in our pajamas. This turned out to be the case for all the normal girls; I was the obviously odd one, already dressed in my running shorts and a tacky T-shirt.

Sometimes I look back on those days and question my own sanity. What was I running from? Or to? Was I so intolerant of my own feelings that I had to literally run away from them? Was I hateful of and masochistic to my own developing body as a young woman? Was I trying to prove something to someone? Or earn my own esteem through my athletic accomplishments?

As I reflect on those days, I often feel sadness and regret for all the parts I missed out on: the normalcy of adolescence, the endless giggling, the widening social interests, and the miscellaneous worrying about typical "end of the world" teenage stuff that I passed up as superficial or uninteresting.

And yet, I also remember that time with gratitude. I appreciate the life lessons my athletic pursuits provided me. Even today, I often tap into whatever kept me going mile after mile after mile.

As a nationally ranked, award-winning long-distance runner, I was a force to be reckoned with. It all started in sixth grade, when I played every sport offered to an elementary-school girl: tennis, basketball, swimming, cheerleading (I guess it's deemed a sport nowadays), and softball. Despite all that, I wanted to run track, too. Given that there was no track team for girls at my school, Coach Hessey invited me to join the boys' track team. I did not understand what I was doing, and I had the wrong shoes to do it in. But Coach just said, "Run," and so I did. I ran for as long and as fast as my legs would carry me. Two months later, he put me on the mile relay team. Four of us passed a baton back and forth, each of us completing one lap around the track. We smashed the school record—three guys and me.

"This girl has talent," said my coach and numerous onlookers.

That summer, Coach Hessey convinced my parents to let me take part in an experiment to see if he was right. Together, we sought real competition, someone other than the boys, someone my own size and gender, for me to race.

"There have to be some girls, somewhere, that can keep up with her, right?" they all wondered.

We travelled throughout the southeast that summer in search of some fast-legged female competition. I raced in the Junior Olympics, and with every meet I won, I then qualified for a larger, more exclusive competition the following weekend. Every round required trips further and further from home. Until, that is, I won the Southeastern Championships. With that, I had come to the end of the track-meet line. I had run out of competition and bested them all.

The following Monday morning, the first day I could sleep in and rest my weary legs, my mother abruptly woke me, shouting, "Ginger! Get up. Put your track uniform on and come downstairs!"

"What now?" I yelled back in frustration. My whole body resisted any such call to order. Besides, my sweat-stained uniform was still lying crumpled on my bedroom floor.

"The phone has not stopped ringing," she replied. "Every local newspaper wants to interview you and take your picture."

Sudden fame was not what I had expected or even wanted. I just wanted to go back to sleep.

But that was only the beginning. I moved through the entire school athletic system–middle school, high school, and college—

running cross-country and track. I broke records and harvested enough medals, trophies, and ribbons to fill a good-sized room. I was voted Most Valuable Runner on the high school varsity cross-country team as a freshman. I was nationally ranked as a top mile-runner, repeatedly hitting sub-five-minute times. I trained in Colorado's high altitude and flew to both coasts to compete nationally. I was even awarded an all-expense-paid trip to compete in the Nationals in San Diego, California.

I wasn't looking ahead. I was just looking down, step by step, having fun, and doing what my body was capable of doing. Meanwhile, the mailbox filled with college scholarship offers. It didn't seem to matter that I was only fourteen.

But then, I grew up; in running years, I grew old. By the time I graduated from college, my knees had started to creak and crack. They slowly stopped being able to bear the repetitive pounding. I had to stop running altogether.

Suddenly, there were no more trophies to earn. Reporters were no longer interested in talking to me. It was now just me, having to face life without the constant pressure to perform and the corresponding glory of yet another victory. I had to find a place for myself in an everyday world that was not timed, recorded, applauded, and rewarded. I had to be my own stopwatch.

The trophies are now packed away, gathering dust in stacked boxes in my basement. I certainly have some good stories to tell my children from it all. However, the best result of all that hard work and all those miles logged are the lessons I internalized and the experiences that still provide a constant supply of resources as I have taken on a different race in mid-life–one that needs just as much stamina and even more strength.

These days, my life feels like strapping on a backpack loaded with bricks each morning. Day in, day out, I swing my feet to the floor to the sound of my blaring alarm/nemesis and grope for that backpack I attempted–some nights successfully, some nights, not so much—to put down while I rested. Some of the heavy bricks I carry are long-term challenges that need daily tending and care, with no immediate outcome or relief in sight. Others are outrageous mistakes I have made myself, times when I dug the hole myself and had to find a way to climb out on my own.

No matter how or when the bricks arrived, they all require that I still take one step forward, again and again, going one day at a time. And so, just like a ten-mile training run, I simply begin. One foot in front of the other. And then another. And then the next one. There is no end in sight; but I just keep going, doing what I know to be the next right action, mile after mile, day after day.

One late November during my sophomore year of high school, our winning team traveled to Pocatello, Idaho, to compete in the cross-country nationals. The forecast predicted frigid temperatures and snow. What was supposed to be an exciting meet for high school runners felt more like climbing Mount Everest in fifty-mile-per-hour winds while being timed.

Aware of the less-than-ideal race conditions, we joked amongst ourselves during our warm-up that there was to be absolutely *no walking*. (We were all such good runners that walking was unheard of—thoroughbreds don't walk.)

After we slogged through the horrendous race, we engaged in our ritualistic post-race wrap-up talk: "How did you do?" or "How do you feel about your race?"

One brave team member dared authenticity and admitted her shame. Cloaked in humor, she braved the truth: "Guys, I had to stop and walk. I couldn't make it up that horrible hill."

We poured endless humiliating laughter upon her.

But now, as I think back on it, I appreciate her honesty. In spite of her athletic prowess and months of preparation, all she could do under the God-forsaken conditions we faced was to stop and walk.

I too find moments, even days, when all I can do is walk. Forget about trophies, medals, and breaking records–hell, I just want to make it to the end of the day. The elements are so powerful and my backpack so full that doing more than simply putting one foot in front of the other–whether to run, walk, or even crawl–is all I can manage.

On the most crushing of days, when I know I have exhibited grit, determination, and integrity, when I have stayed the course of my commitments and responsibilities, I long for a trophy, for that external hardware that says I have won or at least been recognized for my effort.

But I'm an adult now, and we don't have such prizes waiting for us at the finish line. The only medal we receive for completing the day's tasks is the internal satisfaction of a job well done, which can still be important, especially in the face of disappointment and other people's criticism. I must draw my own finish lines now.

I am a long way from being ninety-two pounds thin and having a reputation for being the skinny girl with fast legs. But whatever was inside me then is still inside me today. My steps are bigger now and, dare I say, more important. However, all I must do is exactly what I did then: keep taking the next step, again and again and again. Because, on any given day, that is all any of us can do.

# 3

## *Scripted*

Without any conscious effort on my part, I became the child that plummeted from the confines and comforts of the known. I was the black sheep, the traitor, the one that departed in search of different ground, the one that migrated north geographically and moved left politically. I became unrecognizable to those who shared my origins. I strayed from the familial script.

My Southern family's dynamic can be reduced to one word: control. Lives were scripted for people before they were even conceived. The instructions given and expectations held were more fit to raise mindless robots than human beings. Although I'm sure the emotional constriction predated my grandparents—after all, the dynamics of family legacies are long-lasting and generationally complex—all my memories of it start with them.

I never had much affection for or from my maternal grandmother. She was a formal lady. Cold. Every day, she dressed in her uniform of pearls and ornate dresses, which hid the girdle tightly containing her belly and her rigidity. The upper-right corner of her mouth had a constant slight tick. As the only child of a Methodist minister, I can imagine that a stiff upper lip was a necessary element in her formation; that tick was her only remaining tell.

According to the family story, when my mother was only nineteen, my domineering grandmother, Virginia, picked out my mother's future husband—my father. My mother, Little Virginia, could only comply; she did not know there were other options, or at least ones that would still garner my grandmother's approval. My mother became obediently engaged to my grandmother's chosen man after only six months of dating. She attended the wedding my grandmother had planned. She walked down the aisle, smiling, carrying a bouquet of sweet-smelling gardenias. She said, "I do," to the only life she thought available. Her world had already been scripted;

she was born with her directions in-hand. All she had to do was follow them.

My paternal grandmother was just as controlling. Although cut from a different cloth—one from the red hills of Oklahoma, rather than the demure, lunch-with-the-ladies style—Ruth was also someone you did not cross. If she wanted something done, you did it and you did it her way—at least, if you appreciated her affection.

Mama Ruth, as we called her, kept the details of her personal history secret from us, as if by never discussing it, she had the power to make it go away. The only hint about her past she ever gave was that her father was "kicked by a mule" and subsequently sent to an insane asylum. Ruth was then left all alone to be reared by her brother and his wife, Bootsie.

Mama Ruth's dominant nature was her means of survival. I imagine that her internal state was one of chronic anxiety in anticipation of the next loss. Anxiety is one hell of a drug. Crushing fear ruled her life and the lives of those around her; it was a way of coping with life's unpredictability. Thus, the men in her life–my grandfather and her two sons, the elder being my father—never went anywhere without her. She tagged along on fishing trips, toting homemade pimento cheese sandwiches and still-warm fried chicken. She would not let her world out of her sight, as if her watchful eye could keep them—and her—safe.

And that's just the women in my family. The men were also all molded into pre-prepared roles. My father became a dentist. Just like his father. And his father-in-law. And his brother. My two brothers became dentists. As did my sole male cousin. And, most recently, my nephew and second cousin. Like the women, their lives were designed before they were born.

So what happened with me? Why didn't I just fall in line like I was expected to? After all, I was given the proper family name–the fourth "Virginia" in my maternal line. Why hadn't I been content with the script? Why couldn't I continue the tradition and live a life of young marriage, forever marriage, popping out two or three kids, sitting by the country club pool, socializing with the ladies, supporting my husband's career, going on the latest fad diet? My life would likely have been easier and much more predictable had I followed that path. What was wrong with me that I threw away the playbook and went in search of something vastly different?

I blame my father; it's all his fault. He did not understand what he was doing when he raised me the way he did.

My mother said, "No," to everything: you can't go there, you can't do that, you can't be that.

He said, "Yes."

My mother said, "Marry young so you can have a man take care of you."

My father said, "Get educated and take care of yourself."

My mother asked me, "How many laps is the mile run, again?" even after having watched me run and win it hundreds of times.

My father said, "How far did you run today?"

My mother lived by the script. My father, at least unconsciously, pushed the envelope. I don't think he ever learned how to raise a proper Southern lady.

After dad died without warning, I drifted for decades, lost. Relying on the suffocating script of my Southern roots, with its narrow, limited borders, was out of the question, but without my father, I was without a guide, wandering on my own.

Friends and relatives often asked, "When are you coming home?" I picked up on the love they were trying to communicate in the question, but I always knew my answer: never. My father had given me his drive and energy, and I had to give it free rein, which I couldn't do within the constraints of home. I knew I needed a more expansive plane on which to operate, a life design that was more fitting to my person. So I remained distant from my origins, cast adrift in the wider world.

I made mistakes. Many, in fact. When life is not plotted out for you—or, in my case, if you rebel against the one given to you—you must make it up as you go along. A combination reality show and science project. Trial-and-error with real-life consequences. Less sitcom, more improv.

I will admit that my non-scripted life has been an adventure. I have lived in four different regions of the country. I have been married twice–once to a Midwestern Catholic and once to a New York Jew. I adopted a biracial child and gave birth to a surprise baby girl. I was engaged to a colorful Israeli and now to a long-haired Californian who looks like a cross between Jeff Bridges and Nick Nolte.

Clearly, I am far, far off the familial script. Mine is an ad hoc life, cobbled together by a series of Groundhog Day moments in which I ask the same question again and again: "What the hell do I do next?" Improvising as I go along.

This past spring, I trekked south for my niece's wedding. It was a large, beautiful shindig, one perfectly suited for a Southern princess who had found her prince. While I was ostensibly there to celebrate her milestone, I felt cast adrift in the sea of tumultuous emotions that returning to my homeland inevitably generates. I was suddenly unmoored. I forgot to pack the competent and successful adult I had become; I left her behind in Washington for the weekend.

The blubbering mess of me that was there felt sad that I was witnessing the continuation of our familial script into the next generation: a script of young marriage, forever marriage. They were the picture-perfect Southern couple with their picture-perfect love. Can someone in the family tree please join me in the ranks of the fuck-ups?

At the same time, I felt jealous. Damn it, why couldn't I have done that? My life would have been so much easier, safer, and more predictable, rather than stormy and full of detours. I was suddenly cast back to the angst of my youth, wanting out, yet wanting in, all the while knowing that getting out was my only real option, my only lifeline.

It's still too early to know the future paths of my children. Therapy will be a necessity–that's a given. But like Moses from the book of Exodus, my job was simply to create the path. To break from expectation and throw away the script. To open them to a larger world with limitless possibilities. To continue this metaphor, I will undoubtedly die in the desert, just short of my goal, just shy of the dreamt-of Promised Land. It will be up to my children and grandchildren to enter the land of milk and honey.

They say it's not about how far we go in life; it's about how far we had to go to get there. If I succeeded in transporting my family closer to a legacy of positive emotional growth and psychological freedom even a little, then my life has been worthwhile.

# 4
## *Colorless Love*

I knew to go alone. This film would not do for a girls' night out. I needed to have the space to experience my feelings without having to explain them. And I was right; I cried the whole way through. For two straight hours. I should have brought more Kleenex. The few I had were balled up and torn to shreds by the time I left the theater.

Watching *The Help* was like watching my family portrayed on the big screen. I was immediately swallowed up by the too-real drama, Kathryn Stockett and Hollywood's embellished version of the generations of Southern culture from which I sprang. That movie could have been about my mother's life.

My maternal grandmother was a pristine Memphis belle. She ran the household, but did no housework herself; for that, she had at least three black helpers that I can recall by name.

Ruby was the cook and my favorite. When we children visited, she saw that there were warm Danishes—the ones with the cherry filling and white frosting—on the kitchen table every morning. God, they were good. I would sneakily try to lick my fingers clean to get every last crumb and speck of frosting, until my proper grandmother caught and admonished me for such unladylike behavior.

Thelma was the housekeeper. She donned a white uniform and smiled her toothless grin. And then there was Cherry, the gardener. He minded his own quiet, subservient business, pruning the shrubbery and preserving the illusion that the yard maintained its beauty through the work of some invisible magician.

My grandmother spent her days volunteering at church, playing bridge, and lunching with other ladies like herself. She always began her day with her ongoing battle against her girdle. After she dressed, there came the gentler placement of her fancy flowered hat, followed by the final touch of her long white gloves. Before departing for the day, she left lists of chores for Ruby and Thelma. She would wave to Cherry as she pulled away in her white Dodge Rambler, with its flawless turquoise interior. She was off for her day, leaving other people–black people–to take care of the domestic messes of life: the cooking, the cleaning, the yard work, and the child-rearing. Especially the child-rearing.

My grandmother taught my mother–by words and deeds—to engage life in the same way. Thus, my mother only knew how to duplicate what she had absorbed from her environs—what was now expected of her. A college dropout, my mother married at nineteen and popped out three children before the age of twenty-five. She did not seem to realize that women could do things other than be a housewife, a hostess, and the keeper of black help.

Shortly after the birth of my elder brother, through sheer luck, my mother found and hired Kathryn, known to us as "Tatie."

Tatie was just supposed to work for us. Her loving me was a bonus, a delightful surprise. She would forever after be my black mama.

Every morning around nine o'clock, I listened for her car. The rumble of her barely working jalopy always set my heart at ease. It meant Tatie was here. Whatever I was in the middle of ceased to matter; Tatie was here. I would run down the stairs, abandoning my half-dressed Barbie in favor of my morning hug. I would never miss my morning hug. This big, fat, short, jolly woman always embraced me; her every fold exuded love. I still remember the distinct scent of her skin, which always represented "home."

Tatie was the quintessential maternal force. She made greasy hamburgers for lunch and my favorite pink strawberry cake for my birthday. She fried chicken in Crisco and served it with homemade milk gravy for dippin' on the side. She hummed her favorite gospels tunes in the kitchen. "Oh Happy Day" streamed simultaneously from the radio and her own mouth while she ironed my school uniform into perfect pleats. She watched her midday "stories" while cooking the dinner my mother had assigned. And she chained-smoked. I often stole the cigarettes from her purse and hid them. I couldn't afford to have her die and leave me without her fried chicken and strawberry cake and life-giving embrace. I had to keep her alive because I needed her. She was my black mama, my surprise love.

Once, long ago, too early for my conscious memory, Tatie protected me from my mother's rage. According to family lore, she took me into my bedroom and locked the door. There, she rocked me back and forth, trying to stop my all-too-visible tears and ease my invisible pain. On the other side of the door stood my angry mother. Tatie hollered at her to leave me alone. "Stop hurting my Ginger," she yelled.

Evidently, I had wanted the whole box of chocolate chip cookies, rather than the one serving my mother allowed. In Tatie's opinion, my toddler's desire did not warrant my mother's oversized tantrum. Tatie would see I received justice, even if it was at the expense of her own job. She was my protector.

Another time, when I was in first or second grade, I came home from school one day crying over a history lesson. It was Tatie who noticed my distress and inquired about the source of my tears.

I explained through my labored breath, "I know what you are, Tatie."

She, being the calm, curious, and wise one, replied, "What, honey? What am I? What is Tatie?"

"You're a slave," I wailed, despairing over the newfound status of my beloved black mama.

I don't recall how she reacted to my preposterousness. She may not have responded to it at all, being too busy comforting me amid my brokenhearted realization that someone could even consider mistreating my Tatie. She was not an object. She was not a slave. Not this woman I cherished.

My brother once accidentally shot a hole in the floor with my dad's loaded pistol. Tatie heard the bang from the kitchen and immediately froze in panic. After she had gathered herself, found her voice again, and courageously assessed the bloodless mishap, she scrambled to find a small piece of matching blue carpet from the corner of my dad's overflowing closet. She patched the bullet hole lickety-split, and no one learned of my brother's accident until it was far, far too late to care. Again, Tatie saved a Sullivan. Her quick-thinking resourcefulness so often got us out of jams.

Tatie was also the one who taught my younger brother about the birds and the bees. I wasn't shocked when I heard he named his firstborn after her.

Years later, as an adult living in Chicago, I got an unexpected call from Tatie one day. I instantly knew it was her; I would have recognized that kind, clear voice anywhere. She wanted me to attend church with her as her guest. Her home church was taking a road trip from Nashville to a sister congregation on Chicago's South Side.

A chance to see my Tatie? I wouldn't miss that for the world.

More than one well-meaning friend warned me not to go. "That's not a safe part of town," they said.

I ignored their concerns. Nothing would stop me from going to see my Tatie, even if it meant putting myself in harm's way.

It was a memorable day. Beneath the over-the-top Sunday hats, there was the ritual washing of feet, the slaying of the Devil, the old rhythmic spirituals, the surging energy, and the constant flowing love for God, each other, and the church community gathered there. I had never witnessed such a production before.

After sitting there for what felt like four hours that stretched into eternity, my noisy, empty stomach accompanied the other congregants to supper. It was a spread for the ages: the church basement was filled with fried chicken, macaroni and cheese, mashed potatoes, cornbread, and all the other expected fixin's. Tatie was at home with her people, and I was at home with her.

At least once, Tatie got fed up with our family drama and threatened to quit; I'm sure there were also numerous other times I never knew of. The one time I recall was when my mother's unreasonable demands and accompanying rage finally drove Tatie to her limit. She had had enough. When word of this uprising reached my dad, he abandoned his sedated patients with wide-open mouths in his dental office to rush home and confront the issue face-to-face.

My father, being quite a power to reckon with, told Tatie point-blank, "You cannot quit until my kids are grown and gone. I need you, Tatie, to raise my kids. You cannot go."

Tatie stayed. For another thirty-five years.

She even mothered my mother. There were many days when Tatie lent my mother an ear. Whatever the theatrics of the day, Tatie was her in-house counselor. She offered down-home wisdom alongside her cooking and washing. Sometimes, it seemed like her household tasks were the bonus services, rather than the other way around.

Tatie was the queen bee of our hive, the engine that kept us going. She fed us, cleaned up after us, listened to us, loved us, and kept us from falling apart.

But my love for this woman baffled me and was not without complication. Somehow, I felt I couldn't, shouldn't, love Tatie; after all, she worked for us. Was it okay for me to love her? I was racked with guilt over the possibility that I was betraying my mother and the unspoken "Southern code" by having loving feelings for the black help, for seeing Tatie as a human being, rather than just the employee she was seen as and treated like by others. Something about this discrepancy did not sit well with me, but I didn't understand what it was or why.

Though she was similarly raised by black help, my mother did not have such loving feelings for the help in her household that my brothers and I had for Tatie. We broke the code by loving Tatie when she was just expected to cook and clean. I don't know why or how it happened; it seemed natural that if someone had such a valued place in my life, then strong feelings would naturally accompany that attachment.

On one occasion, we had company over for supper. As the guests effusively complimented the meal, I sat there and observed my mother receive all the praise, as if she had been the one laboring in the hot kitchen all day. As my mother graciously smiled a plastic smile and said, "Well, thank you," I grew increasingly disturbed.

"Am I the only one who sees that this whole thing is a sham?" I wondered. "The only one who sees that the Emperor really has no clothes?" I became more and more uncomfortable, trying to understand and work through the craziness playing out right in front of me. I knew the truth, and I could not contain it. I felt that Tatie now needed my protection; I had to stand up for what I thought was right or at least true. I didn't yet have the adult capacity to tolerate wrongness.

When I could no longer help myself, before I could even ponder the consequences, I blurted out, "Tatie made everything."

The conversation stopped in its tracks, and all eyes were suddenly on me. How dare I break the code? The satisfaction I felt in that moment of honesty ended with my mother's wrath later that night—after the guests had left, of course.

But it was worth it. I'm glad I spoke up. I was then, and I still am now. Someone needed to verbalize the truth: that hard work done in love should not go unnoticed and should be spoken of honestly. Tatie cooked because it was her job to cook. But she cooked with love because she loved us.

Another thing that puzzled me was how so much love could come from someone who had so little. Tatie had all the responsibilities of running our household, yet none of the outward privileges of being the adored matron.

I peeked once; I saw her weekly paycheck sitting on the corner cupboard in the kitchen. I got to see exactly how much Tatie was being paid for her domestic—as well as unspoken and unpaid emotional—labor. It was less than a few hundred dollars a week in 1970s dollars. It must have been close to the poverty line.

From my parents' perspective, her low pay was justified because they gave her our old hand-me-downs, things we no longer wanted or needed. I occasionally had the chance to visit her modest, run-down house on the other side of town—the black side of town. It was stocked with recognizable items from our house or my dad's dental office. I guess my parents considered her getting our leftovers as a benefit of the job. The condescension both angered and saddened me.

Another "job perk" was that Tatie could bring her grandson to work with her whenever she needed to. From our perspective as children, Tatie simply came with an occasional playmate. He was our friend, even though he was shy and we couldn't get him to talk much.

It was also not lost on me that race, racism, and separateness were as much a part of her black identity as they were for my family's white one. When I turned eighteen, my parents threw a huge surprise birthday party for me. As usual, Tatie was the one behind the scenes who made it all happen. During the party, she peeped around the corner from the kitchen to gaze at the crowd gathered in the living room. When she spotted a lone black girl among the young white faces, she abruptly exclaimed, "There is a black girl in this house!"

"Yes," my mother explained, quickly pulling Tatie back into the kitchen so that the guests would not hear her, "that's Linda. She's one of Ginger's friends from school."

Tatie would have nothing of the sort. "No black girl belongs in this house!" she stated with resolve.

For once, we ignored her. My friend of a different skin color was welcome.

Still, Tatie's self-imposed segregation confused me. My love for Tatie was colorless; race had nothing to do with our relationship, at least from my point of view. She had long since risen far beyond the role of mere household help in my eyes. Yet she wanted to stay in her humble place, the one that Southern culture had assigned her race for generations. Unbeknownst to her, she would lose this battle, at least with me. Years later, I would adopt and raise a black son of my own.

Aside from being the recipient of her love, I learned a few things from Tatie. In fact, she turned my entire world upside down and gave me a perspective that has forever influenced my internal landscape. From her, I learned about being the underdog, about having resilience, backbone, heart, and compassion. I learned about class discrepancy and unspoken institutionalized racism. I learned that there is more to life than a silver spoon and a white cloth-napkin lunch. I learned that life is not about what you have, but about making the most of what you have. I learned that someone with so little could be enough for the heart and the soul. I learned that true love takes us by surprise; it cannot be dictated. It blossoms where it is nurtured.

Many years now separate me from my Barbies and plaid school skirts. Regardless, it would do my heart good now and again to revisit the green-and-yellow kitchen of my childhood and watch Tatie make her juicy fried chicken while I tell her the specifics of my day. As with everything else that has ever happened, I do not know what my life might have been like without my unexpected love for Tatie and her love for me. The thought of my childhood without her consistent love—hidden in Southern cooking and enthusiastic affection—is unfathomable.

Before Tatie passed, I made a point of visiting her on every occasion I went back to Tennessee. Each time I entered her simple residence, I was struck by that same scent, that same joy, that same feeling of love. I would inevitably be moved to tears by the sight of my Tatie, my home on some subterranean, cellular level. I would try to hold back these feelings, at least until I left. Then, they would pour forth uncontrollably. I was saying good-bye to my black mama, at least until the next time I made it back South. I knew she would not be around much longer.

Tatie died recently. At her home-going service, her family sat in the middle front row. Six generations of love crowded the pews behind. We, her white kids, assembled in the front row to the left side. We were all family, despite our different skin color, all gathered to celebrate the life of one extraordinary woman.

Rest in peace, Tatie. Wherever you are, it's your time now. Put your tired feet up, turn up those gospel tunes, light a cigarette, and let the universe love you as you loved so many of us. For you are my Tatie, my black mama.

# 5
## *Show Me the Food*

"Mom! Mooooooommmmmm! He's doing it again!" I screamed down the stairs, desperately hoping I could wake her. I did not want to be the one to clean it up. Not again.

We all knew the drill; it was as certain as the turn of the seasons. We would have dinner—or rather, a feast—at grandma's, followed by a dessert of warm, homemade blackberry cobbler topped with vanilla ice cream. My little brother would always eat more than his share. Who could blame him when it was a choice between a delicious second helping and guilt for refusing our grandmother's offering? Then, later that night, he would inevitably puke up blue vomit all over his bedsheets at three o'clock in the morning.

My brother's ritual–with its corresponding messy consequences—was commonplace at our house, but he was not the only one who struggled with moderation.

Food was the dominant method of communicating love in our family. It came in abundance, was deep-fried, and was passed around with extra helpings always available. Not just comfort food, the food itself was comfortable, snug in blankets of breading and fat. But as plentiful as the food was, it was no substitute for the more essential emotional nutrients. No matter how much we packed our mouths and filled our stomachs, the heart's hunger remained unsatisfied. There were just not enough emotional goodies to go around. We were all hungry for affection and attention, yet due to its sporadic supply, we never knew when more would be dished up.

But food? Shit, food was available in platefuls, and we all partook, even if it led to self-destructive weight gain, high cholesterol, and middle-of-the night vomit.

Even the non-humans in our family were overfed. My father's parents had a Dalmatian named Dolly that was as wide as she was tall. Every afternoon, my grandmother Ruth would cook the dog's dinner. Rather than go to the cupboard and grab a cup of the usual Purina kibble, my grandmother made a full meal for this elite animal. Naturally, Dolly dined Southern: fried chicken plucked from the bone, green beans cooked with ham hock, mashed potatoes with melted cheese on top, plus two homemade biscuits with butter and strawberry jam on the side. Dolly ate this plated meal every single day. I tease you not.

One day, my younger brother–the one that regularly threw up the blackberry cobbler in the middle of the night when we was a youngster—stopped by my grandparents' house while he was out running around town. He chatted with my grandmother while she cooked what he thought was dinner for her and my grandfather. To his surprise, she dished up a plate and asked him, "Temp, can you run this meal out to Dolly for me?"

Dumbfounded, Temp eyed the gourmet spread, realizing that this dog was about to have a better meal than what he had enjoyed all day. For her part, Dolly simply lay in her outdoor quarters, waiting for her afternoon feast. The last thing the barely walking canine needed was another buttered biscuit with homemade jam.

So instead of delivering the meal as instructed, Temp sat down in the backyard and secretly indulged. I have no idea what Dolly ate for dinner that night, but I do know my brother was full and happy. In our family, you learned to take love—and food as the equivalent of love—wherever you could find it.

As clear as this message was, even as a little girl, I knew something about using food as emotional currency didn't seem right.

I recall countless large family gatherings where endless amounts of food were passed around freely, yet not a single word of meaningful conversation ever went alongside it. "Mmm. This sure is good," was about the extent of any verbal exchange.

No matter how tasty the food was, the emotional emptiness always left me longing for more. Even with a cleaned plate in front of me, I pulled my chair back from the dining table still starving and unfulfilled. My young, yearning heart wondered what the point was of this full-blown charade. Why bother with the shopping, the hours of cooking, and a kitchen that looked like it had been hit by a tornado, when what was really needed was satisfying emotional food? I wanted to stand up and scream, "Does anyone here have a real thought or feeling? Am I the only one that wants—and needs— connection?"

But I never dared.

I was too cowardly—or too well-trained. Instead, I learned to swallow my unhappiness and my desire for deeper relationships along with the green beans, mashed potatoes, and pecan pie.

When I left home and wandered north, I was banking on a geographical cure. "Surely," I thought, "Northerners don't merely pretend happy. Surely, they talk with substance." But, oh, was I wrong. I discovered that superficiality is not restricted to the South; it is a human commonality that crosses all cultures.

I have a former in-law who, I swear, epitomized the phrase "psychotic chatter." That woman talked incessantly about everything while saying absolutely nothing that would lead to an emotional connection between herself and another person. She never even looked up to see if the other party was paying attention. Let's just say I did a lot of knitting during those years.

Over time, I grew to appreciate and embrace my need for in-depth dialogue, rather than deem it "too much" or as a need that could not be satisfied. I acquired the verbal and emotional skills to engage in deeper conversations and found willing participants who were crazy enough to choose the same. As a more fulfilled human being, I, ironically, became more tolerant of small talk. I began to see its value as a conversation-starter and a rapport-builder.

But, at least for me, pleasant chitchat will always just be an appetizer. I need to know a hardy course is coming next. Tantalize my taste buds, but bring me something of substance. Dish up something I can put a fork in, something that will stick to my bones. Don't just leave me with talk of the weather and the latest office gossip. I want to know what stirs your heart. What you have lost. What you dream about. What keeps you up at night and what gets you up in the morning. Then, and only then, we can truly dine over an authentic meal. Together, we can indulge our non-negotiable need for genuine human connection.

Yes, that. Pass me that, please. I don't care if it comes on a flimsy paper plate. I will feast like a queen.

# 6
## *First Day of School*

I remember looking around and counting; the white straps were easily detectable under the pale-yellow cotton uniform button-down blouses. I think there were two of us—two middle-school girls that did not yet wear a bra. I didn't even own one, because I didn't need one. I had no use for it, no burgeoning breasts that needed support. That first day of seventh grade at Nashville's premier all-girls prep school was quite daunting to my prepubescent self. I was not prepared for this abrupt leap into womanhood. Suddenly, I was cast into a foreign land and was made alien with no time to prepare.

"Take me back!" my confused mind protested. I would never have said such a thing aloud, but I desperately wanted to return to the familiar territory I knew and had conquered. Just three months prior, I had been safely snuggled within the confines of my small, private elementary school. Not only did I fit in, I was at the top of the heap: hardworking, athletic, outgoing–all the right ingredients to be a likeable presence in such a simple world. I could be myself while being accepted by others. It was a good arrangement.

So what had happened?

The game had changed, and I had no clue how to play it now.

I was lost in the environs of pleated uniforms, makeup, and social chatter. I could not compete in this strange new ambience; I did not have the skill set or the social, emotional, and bodily goods. I was out of place, like an Eskimo dropped into the Mojave Desert. My system was in shock, and my identity thrown into crisis. Thin, wordless, pretending—as a form of protection—to want and need nothing. I was locked inside my preteen self.

Mind you, I played by the rules. I got up every day and buckled my blue-and-green plaid kilt; donned my ankle-length bobby socks and black-and-white Oxford saddle shoes; double-checked that my meticulously crafted homework was tucked away in my backpack, ready to make my teachers smile; and—the most important element in my daily preparation ritual–I swallowed any feelings I might dare express. My behavior was perfectly compliant; my masked facade fully disguised any underlying emotional content. I did exactly what was expected of me. I was a nose-to-the-grindstone model student. No need to waste time worrying about me.

But inwardly, I was a wreck. In this societal factory that was in the business of producing perfect ladies, I felt I had no value. My energy and offerings of the previous year seemed unimportant, even non-existent, in this land of up-and-coming young women. I was not one of "them," and who I had thought I was had suddenly become obsolete. Since I did not have the wherewithal or the goods— the social skills, the beauty, the glamour, the breasts—to be among them, I didn't even attempt to fit in or compete. It was futile.

But, shit, I needed some kind of survival plan. And I needed it fast.

I went underground and became anonymous. I folded into my own world, escaping to the dark, quiet corners of my innermost caverns. I remained out of the limelight, not wanting my oddness to be detected, my inferiority exposed. My plan was to keep attention at bay, to do just enough, well enough, to be left alone. I was certain my tactic to withstand adolescence would be a success.

And it was. For years. No one saw my pain. My outwardly cooperative behavior kept others unconcerned about me. No one worries about a well-behaved student who makes good grades.

I was safe.

Until I wasn't.

Unbeknownst to me, when I awoke one morning in the spring of my freshman year of high school—my routine of the plaid skirt and saddle shoes automated by then—I had no idea that this day would be a turning point.

We sat on the school's front lawn for the annual end-of-year picnic. All five hundred-some-odd of us girls, looking generic in our uniform of sameness. The air smelled of freshly mown grass and newly blossomed magnolias, as it always does in a Southern spring.

The headmistress droned on, talking nonsense about the highlights of the soon-to-be-over school year. I tuned it all out, more focused on the anxiety pounding in my chest, a state I knew well and had to manage whenever social situations were forced upon me. I just wanted to go back to class, back to my comfort zone—a domain I had long-since mastered.

The headmistress then began to announce the names of students who had achieved academic honors for the year.

"More boring chitchat," I told myself.

Mind you, I already had plenty of hardware for my athletic prowess. I was used to that kind of recognition. But when the headmistress called my name for academic achievement, I was not the only one who was surprised.

"Has there been some mistake? Who is this girl?" The open-mouthed crowd seemed to be asking the same questions I was asking myself.

I did not even suspect that I was smart compared to the other students; I just worked hard and kept my head down. My focus was always on putting one foot in front of another, in classwork as in running. And because I had kept myself invisible, my peers had not identified me as bright, either. But now I had been exposed. My secret was out. I could no longer hide.

I shyly walked forward to receive my award, a green blanket with a sewn-on emblem of the school's crest. Head down in embarrassment, I knew my cover had been blown. I wasn't sure what to do now that my strategy of obscurity had failed. I was in need of a new game plan to maneuver my frightened heart through life.

In the decades to come, I would attempt and abort many a scheme to steer my way. Whether through humor, self-deprecation, grandiosity, masochism, running away, shutting down, or staying in a toxic or codependent relationship, I was insistent in my belief that I needed some kind of action to survive, as opposed to bravely facing the dark, raw places within. But none of these approaches were successful over the long haul. Inevitably, I would have to unearth my authentic self to find a place in the world, a place where I not only belonged, but also one that offered peace to my tattered heart.

Looking back now, I admit it's possible that I had it all wrong. During those long-ago school days, maybe I really had fit in after all. Perhaps what I had struggled with was on the inside, not how others experienced me on the outside. Maybe I just needed someone to take the time to see me and let me know as much. To reach in, find me, and tell me, "Yes, you have a place here. You matter."

That gap between who we think we are and how others see us can be a wide one. The discrepancy between these two visions can be so great we might miss the abundance right in front of us. I missed it back then in the halls of high school, and I regret that.

But with that loss comes a chance now, in this moment, to embrace life as it is. For the table is large, and the banquet, plenty. And bra or no bra, there is a place for all.

# 7
## *Drop-Off Magic*

"I'll pick you up in a few hours," my mother yelled as I opened the chain-link gate and skipped up the cracked sidewalk. I barely heard her words, much less cared about them. I was solely focused on the steps ahead that led to the front door—the door that led to the house of love.

I always looked forward to those afternoons with my great aunt, Bootsie. Her given name was "Una," but with a name like that, even she knew she needed a nickname. We called her Bootsie, though no one seems to recall why. At least, no one cared to explain it to me. I didn't care what she was named; I adored her.

"Come in! Come in!" she would enthusiastically greet me when she opened the front door. "I've been waiting for you."

My heart was always warmed by Bootsie's fervent welcome. Once through the door and inside her hospitable home decorated in shades of dusty rose and jade green, I was swallowed in her affection. Her wrinkled face and folds of fat would embrace my skinny self, just as her vital spirit greeted me. My afternoon of homespun magic had begun.

First on the agenda was rolling out the biscuit dough on Bootsie's white-flour-coated kitchen counter. We made the Southern staple from scratch and punched lard-infused circles in the dough with an old-fashioned, dented biscuit cutter. Bootsie's biscuits were of the thick, flaky variety, the kind that, when joined with a pat of butter, seemed to go on for days, like hot lava pouring from a volcano.

While the biscuits took their time baking, we laughed at the flour now covering our clothes. Laughter quickly turned to dance, and the kitchen became our stage. Bootsie's infectious spirit enlivened the room and, more importantly, me.

Next up on our afternoon agenda was fashion design. Our feet peddled Bootsie's squeaky sewing machine as we created fanciful outfits for my poor, naked baby doll. To what glamorous party my doll would wear her newly designed attire, I had no clue. But it didn't matter. I was happily in the magical land of Bootsie, who was the magician creating everything in this fantastical world my mother had unknowingly dropped me off in.

During those afternoons, time stopped. I relaxed, both body and heart, into the fullness of the moment. But then, suddenly, the clock would remind me of its harsh ability to betray. My mother would be there, knocking at the door, beckoning me to leave Bootsie's house of unbounded love.

The story goes that Bootsie could never have children. Back then, they called it "barren"—a shameful scarlet "B"—instead of the now commonly known and openly discussed "infertility." Her husband had died a few days before I was born, so, left widowed and childless, directionless and bereft, Bootsie turned to me. Through sheer luck—or perhaps fate—I became the fortunate recipient of all her fondness. Loss can do that: make us look for new vessels to hold our hearts. But Bootsie's and my arrangement was mutual; she needed to love, and I needed love.

True female love and affection was a rarity in my family. It was generally too cluttered, too tied up in layers of expectation and dictation of how and what a female should be and, more tellingly, become. Messages of less-than-ness were always implied and sometimes even spoken aloud: "You can't do that," or, "That's a man's job," or, "You can be a dental hygienist, but not a dentist." However they were relayed, old scripts were still being used to shape women in my family. They were a biscuit cutter of a different kind, one with a more lasting edge.

But to me, Bootsie offered the refreshment of creativity and play, of freedom from a given script. She was a nurturing maternal figure that opened me, rather than closed me, to possibility. She expanded my world, rather than limiting it. She taught me to be big, rather than small. To be more, not less.

Bootsie died while I was in college. Sadly, it was a non-event. The woman I loved had been slowly disappearing for quite some time. Her mind had already vanished, leaving her body before her body was done living. We called her "crazy," as the more accurate and sophisticated diagnosis of Alzheimer's was not yet commonly understood parlance. I imagine her caretaking relatives were simply relieved that her body had finally surrendered. Her graveside service was small, with only a few attendees. Unfortunately, I couldn't be among them.

All these decades later, I wish I had Bootsie's biscuit recipe. My attempts at duplicating it yield creations that are more like rock-hard hockey pucks than her perfect buttered circles. I do have a sewing machine, but it sits in my musty basement, probably in need of a tune-up, just waiting for me to crank it up and cobble together some new whimsical designs.

But I dance in the kitchen. Every chance I get, in fact. Even though my easily embarrassed kids tell me to stop. But I never do. And I never will.

However, such outward signs of Bootsie's impact on my little-girl self are immaterial. What was most valuable about my relationship with Bootsie was that she saw me. To my pint-sized self, my full-sized aunt was humongous. She was the source of my drop-off magic, my surprise dose of attention and love.

Love does that, you know. It shows up, often in unanticipated, wondrous ways. As a young girl, I needed that. Heck, I still desire that. I imagine you might as well. We just need to spot love's gifts, even when—especially when—it's not so obvious where they can be found.

Perhaps on a good day, as the circle goes around, we can be the ones extending love's reach to an unexpecting someone. Who knows? Maybe it's in the giving of love that magic truly abides.

# 8
## *Crazy Love*

"You girls have to be back by supper tomorrow night!" shouted the heavyset, domineering camp director at our retreating backs.

"Yes, ma'am," we compliantly and automatically replied.

But for once—just for that one day—we didn't give a shit about what she said. We were out of there, free, as if on a thirty-six-hour pass from prison, our headlights pointed south.

Honey Rock Camp is about eight hours north of Chicago in the lush Northwoods of Wisconsin, somewhere between civilization and the Canadian border. We three twenty-something girls had willingly given our summers to the place. In exchange for our hard work, early hours, and missed opportunities that most young-adult women would surely prefer, we were earning summer college credits, and we well knew of our sacrifice. By about halfway through the summer, we were itching for a break and—more importantly—some loving. To hell with the icy-cold lake swims, the bland camp food, and the untouched lips. We wanted some age-appropriate action, and we were now headed south to get it.

We also had more in common than the decision to spend our summer of 1986 in the Wisconsin wilderness: we were all in love. Carrie, Diane, and I were aching to connect with our men, who were all just outside Chicago, holding our hearts. Why else would a person drive sixteen hours to only spend twenty in our destination? We were young fools, entangled in love's tentacles, the victims of her seductive, irresistible grip.

John and I had been together for about four years by that point. We had gone to neighboring high schools and had both taken someone else to the spring dance sophomore year. Despite that, our mutual attraction was undeniable, and after our plans for the prom had been solidified, but before they could be carried out, we were talking on the phone for hours each evening. We did not verbalize it, but we both wished we were going to the dance together, rather than with our respective invited dates. We ultimately kept our original commitments, but our infatuated eyes remained locked on each other all night. Within days, we made our relationship public, and four years later, we were still going strong–me and my intelligent, bad-boy wrestler, a Matt-Damon-look-alike with a square jaw, blue eyes, and an irresistible puppy-dog smile.

It was that love that propelled me down I-94 that summer, mad with the thought of seeing him. Carrie, Diane, and I made a beeline south, changing drivers just often enough to avoid falling asleep at the wheel. Surprisingly, we garnered only one speeding ticket, though we certainly deserved more. Too many hours later, we finally arrived at our longed-for destination: in the arms of our respective men. We were home.

With an arm glued around her soon-to-be-fiancé, Carrie announced, "If we're going to make our deadline back at camp, we'll need to meet back here at ten a.m. tomorrow."

Diane and I grimaced, already anticipating the end of our all-too-short rendezvous, when we would have to return to the Northwoods of Wisconsin and the aching emptiness in our hearts. Then, realizing that the clock was ticking, we all quickly scattered with our matched loves.

Even the shabbiest of one-star motels was beyond our budgets as poor college students, so for the next twenty hours, I lay beside my high-school-turned-college-boyfriend in the haven that was his 1960s Volkswagen bus, one of those ugly, burnt-orange hippie vans. Fortunately, I didn't give a shit about my environment, couldn't have cared less about the aesthetics or the amenities. All that mattered was that I was nestled in his strong arms—safe, warm, loved, and never to be happier.

We initially parked the van in a neighborhood park. Then, trying to remain inconspicuous to roaming police officers, we moved to a parking lot behind a grocery store for the remainder of the night. We figured we'd give the early rising stockers something to talk about as they neatly placed Campbell's tomato soup cans on the shelf.

The night hours became those of early morning. Sleep was not on our agenda. After all, we only had a few precious minutes together before the camp director put out a search warrant for us, and we sure as hell weren't going to waste our valuable time unconscious, lost in some dream world, apart from each other. Separation was coming soon enough. We were living our dream, and we dared not squander it to sleep.

As the minutes ticked by and unwelcome sunlight crept through the bus's windows, the happiness of our reunion slowly drifted into a growing sadness. Our intimate feast was ending.

As a last-minute gesture, showing feelings he didn't know how to speak directly, John put on Paul Young's song, "Every Time You Go Away." I imagine it was his attempt at either reassuring my anxious heart or warding off his own pain. Unfortunately, it didn't work; I still cried halfway back to camp.

First love—it's the only experience in our lives when we give away every last piece of our hearts in reckless abandon. There is nowhere we won't go, nothing we won't do for that innocent, untainted connection.

Reflecting on that journey we young women took through the dark Wisconsin night, there is no word to describe such a trip other than "crazy." Who would drive sixteen hours only to spend twenty looking up at the ceiling of a VW van?

I did.

And I would do it again if I had the chance. The opportunity to say, "Fuck it. I'm outta here. For the next thirty-six hours, I'm throwing caution to the wind, taking a chance, and acting ludicrous, all in search of life's nectar: the sweetness of innocent, unadulterated love."

I am middle-aged now. My heart is wiser. It knows better, identifies such youthful love as, well, just that: young. Naïve. Unreal. Untested. Fragile. Like a return to the womb, it is an endorphin bath. It allows us to suckle again at an endless untainted bond. Yet it has also not been deepened by life's many daily demands into a solid vintage that can be sustained for decades.

We only get one chance to love for the first time. Just one stint on the new playground of our young, hungry bodies. One opportunity to give away our hearts without having to protect them behind cautious walls. One window in which we can love freely without the foresight to understand that disappointment is inevitable and heartbreak likely.

By now, I've been on love's rollercoaster many times. I know its thrills, and I also realize its all-too-frequent outcome.

Falling in love is easy. Learning to stay in love while making love work...well, that's a whole other ballgame.

Thus, I'm sure glad I took that crazy trip south on Interstate 94 back in the summer of 1986. It stands as a memory of rebellious joy—like eating dessert first. It reminds me that sweet delight is possible if I keep putting my heart out there. All I must do is take love up on the next ride, the one that ends in my heart's satisfaction.

# 9
## *Happily, Ever After*

"Not my daughter! She will not have to like pink!" I vowed to myself long before I had a daughter of my own. I was adamant that she would have full choice of the color-wheel spectrum. She would not be forced into pink.

As the prospect of having children and raising a girl became a possibility, my childhood resistance to the color pink and the culture of princesses hardened even more. Cultural norms be damned; I would not encourage such worn-out, restrictive stereotypes for my child.

But I had a daughter. And as I should have expected, she liked pink. Payback, no doubt, for my stubborn stand against gender formulas.

As children ourselves, we harbor fantasies about what our future offspring might be like. When I was a childless twenty-something, my future daughter was unencumbered by all I had struggled against. She could pursue her heart's desire from its widest range. Unlike me, she wouldn't have to fight to carve out a separate identity, to find and become her true self. She would enjoy freedom.

As the first female in my Southern family to not follow the traditional path of her foremothers, I had crossed the threshold, broken the glass ceiling. College beyond the Mason-Dixon line; a respectable, intellectual career with my own livable salary; athletic accomplishments written up in the newspaper–these were all oddities for women in my gene pool. But they wouldn't be for my daughter. She would bask in the endless opportunities I had fought for and won.

And for God's sake, she would not have to like the color pink.

She would be free to run and play without stopping to be the nurturing one. She would be unrestrained, footloose to explore all of who she is minus the subtle and not-so-subtle messages of limitation due to her sex. She could discover her talents without the fear of disappointing the determiners of "what a girl should be." She would be her own arbiter, powerful and binding. The world would be her oyster, and I was thrilled to provide her such liberty.

Or so I thought.

By the time my daughter was five, she was as coordinated and as smart as any child—boy or girl—in her Montessori class, yet pink pervaded me. Everything had to be pink. Mama Ruth would have been so pleased.

We played Barbies and princesses. We bought fairy wands and spread sparkling fairy dust everywhere. We did pliés and chasséd across the floor in our mother-daughter ballet class. We read stories that ended with "… and they lived happily ever after." We got our nails painted. We frolicked while playing dress-up and went shopping.

"What am I doing?" I asked myself. My inner feminist wanted to revolt. I no longer recognized myself. Again and again I wondered, "Is this some unknown, suppressed version of myself? Is this *my* daughter?"

Without encouraging or force-feeding it, there it was: that love of all things pink and "girly" that I had so loathed as a child. To my disappointment and surprise, the princess had surfaced like a jack-in-the-box that had popped open automatically. She must reside somewhere on the X chromosome.

I could have done the same thing that was done to me, only in reverse: I could have refused her her choices and forced her to be what I wanted her to be. I could have told her what she liked and didn't like. I could have dressed her in the manner I preferred. I could have cut her hair to my liking.

But I couldn't do that. I wouldn't do that. I know how those shoes feel, and I have spent way too much time and money on the therapy couch to cram her toes into footgear that is wrong-sized.

So—internally kicking and screaming—I surrendered. I bought pink everything, read and reread *Pinkalicious*, and entered the fantasy of being a princess in fairyland.

Which brings me to another point.

How long do I let this—the myth of life turning out happily ever after—go on? My life certainly hasn't unfolded like that, nor has that of anyone else I know. Either I'm in the wrong crowd or my limited sample accurately reflects truth—the reality that princes don't show up to save the day, that things don't always turn out happily ever after, that wands aren't magical, and that, sometimes, the shoe just doesn't fucking fit.

Do I really want my daughter to buy into this lie? Do I really need to set her up for the biggest disappointment of her life by colluding with this enchanted—but patently false—fantasy? Can I really swallow this delusion enough to pretend gleefully for her sake?

Perhaps the tellers—and, later, the writers—of fairy tales weren't thinking about the psychological development of prepubescent girls and the need to prepare them for real life and real-life expectations. Or were they? Maybe they were all-too-aware of the harshness of life. Maybe they were encouraging the prospect of dreams as a counterbalance to all the cruelty these girls would encounter. That despite wicked stepmothers and sadistic witches, hope can and does prevail. Forces of evil can be overcome, and love wins out over pain every time. I mean, kids must read and reread these fairy tales for a reason. Fifty million Brothers Grimm fans can't be wrong.

From that point of view, I don't have the heart to crush my daughter's hopeful magic. I can't be the one to tell her at such a tender age that life is about suffering, that dreams sometimes falter, that grief and loss are inevitable, and that nothing lasts forever. So, I will get up tomorrow, and the next day, and the next, and perpetuate the fantasy of Cinderella at the ball in her gorgeous size-two gown, wearing glass slippers, dancing the night away with her dapper prince.

And before I can bat an eye, my daughter will be fifteen, and the fantasies of fairyland will have faltered on their own through life's school of hard knocks. She will then come to me in the fullness of her teenage angst and woes and tell me how harsh life really is.

And then, it will be my turn to offer the fantasy–or the reality– that life also contains the good, that miracles can occur, that love often comes in unexpected ways at unexpected times, and that it is well worth it to keep one's dreams alive.

As parents, we all want to give our children more than was given to us. For me, I guess that means that, today, I play Barbies and buy pink, knowing that tomorrow, my daughter may well choose to wear black, be in a rock band, and have multiple piercings in places I don't want to know about.

I must cultivate the emotional flexibility to tolerate her being whatever she needs to be for herself in that moment—some version of an Existential Gumby. I must be able to give voice to the totality of life's many faces: to uphold the hopeful and the good, to be there for the inevitable letdown, and still be willing to put my heart out there again and wish upon a star.

# 10

## *The Magic Kingdom*

"Are you sure you want to do this?" I asked my kids one last time before I hit the "Enter" button, which would transform the idea of this vacation into a non-refundable reality. I was secretly hoping they would tell me they had come to their senses and would rather spend Spring Break at a quiet beach resort where they would wait on me hand and foot, attending to my need for rest and peace.

Instead, they screamed, "YES!" in unison, barely even looking up from whatever screen held their attention in that moment.

I sighed deeply and forced my finger to press the button. We were going.

This parenting thing is hard. Damn hard.

On the upside, at least I would finally be removed from the Bad Mother list on this particular issue. It had taken me until my kids were teenagers to check the box for that mandatory childhood trip to Disney World. I'm not sure why or how we had waited so long; either central Florida had been low on my radar or I had been downright resistant. But Mickey and Minnie proved to be eternally patient, and now, at long last, we would answer their siren song.

"At least the weather will be great," I tried to convince myself. "The sunshine alone will be worth thousands after the winter we've had in Washington." Self-deception is welcome when facing desperation. It's a coping skill. And I was desperate: crowds, long lines, and lots of noise are not high on my list of favorite experiences.

After making the commitment, the three of us immersed ourselves in all-things-Disney. After all, you can't go without a plan. Which park on which day? How many rides can you get on the Fast-Pass+? Would we need lunch reservations? Could we even still get reservations at this late date—four months ahead of time? Stay on-campus or off? Rental car or Uber? The fucking decisions were never-ending. I longed for someone to just make it all happen for me. Like magic.

So, after all that preparation and anticipation, did "The Place Where Dreams Come True" live up to the hype? Were those picturesque, smiley-faced ads genuine?

Hardly.

What was supposed to be a land of endless thrills and smiles—life in highly crafted perfection—was nothing more than trumped-up normality, a fancy version of the everyday. You can glamorize the princess, but she remains a human being.

Rather than foolproof happiness, most of what I observed during those four fun-filled days was overly tired, screaming toddlers being forced to smile for the camera "just one more time"; exhausted parents who looked like they were on an expensive, never-ending walking marathon; and endless crowds casting envious glances at the FastPass+ line. I think I got my money's worth in people-watching alone. It was a pricey sociological experiment.

At one point, my daughter and I gave up our planned agenda in favor of "princess spotting." It seemed more entertaining than standing in a line for two hours at Space Mountain, and it proved to be so much fun that we would like to recommend it as a new activity at Disney World. We veered away from Tomorrowland back to Fantasyland just to snap pictures of random little girls decked out from head-to-at-least-knee in perfect princess costumes, all in hopes of actually becoming said princess (attracting a dapper prince probably came a distant second). Although their gowns were most likely cheap, Chinese-made knockoffs, these girls proudly strutted in their frocks as though they were on their way to a real ball to dance with Prince Charming. The shoes tended to be on the casual side—a major fashion faux pas for true princesses, I imagine—but hell, this is the twenty-first century, and Disney World is not easy on the feet. Mickey wears big, round, cushioned shoes for a reason. Most of these young princesses even had their hair done, often greased back into a tight bun with a faux diamond tiara on top, just in case anyone should mistake them for an ordinary child.

My daughter and I were impressed by their determination, if not downright jealous of their style. We wanted to shed our shorts and T-shirts for their more glamorous (imagined) lives, lives in which all their dreams were guaranteed to come true.

Instead, we settled for Reality Disney, which included:

- A teenage son/brother who spent one of the days hunkered down in the hotel room and ordering pizza, rather than experiencing the Magic Kingdom.
- An angry mother (me) who stupidly reminded him how much money this trip had cost her.
- A rainy day at Epcot with cheesy, overpriced Mickey Mouse ponchos and useless, flimsy, soaked paper maps.
- A deaf Uber driver who gave our grouchy, tired selves cold water, breath mints, and a warm smile at the end of a long day.
- A must-buy action photo from Splash Mountain—the woman in front's hilarious flying Kramer hair, a bonus.
- Countless rollercoaster rides, all of which guaranteed motion sickness for me. "Where is the closest vomit bag?" I often inquired, realizing that I had overlooked this necessity in the packing plan. These God-awful experiences brought my daughter sheer joy, though: "Let's go again, Mom!" she shouted more than once as I stared at her, ghost-white.

You get the idea.

Even in a make-believe, plastic-coated world, reality wins. We are still stuck being human, experiencing the full range of human realities.

Did the kids and I have a perfect vacation in a perfect place? Absolutely not. We fought. We made up. We laughed. We sang loudly. We ate too much. We spent too much. We embarrassed ourselves. We embarrassed each other. Standing in seemingly endless lines, with sweat dripping down our backs and our faces, we were miserable. Yet, in unexpected moments of my son's spontaneous humor, we also peed our pants.

Our adventure was far from ideal, and it was wonderful.

Life demands inclusivity–we need all things good to exist alongside all things not-so-good. Even Walt Disney himself could not design a completely flawless world.

Now if I could just get some fairy with a magic wand to zap that into my thick head, I'm sure I could walk off happily into the sunset. But I guess that, too, ain't gonna happen. Rather, I must keep learning and living the hard way, each day and in each moment, with life itself as my best–and only–teacher.

# 11
## *No Stopping Now*

I was a misfit from day one. Although born in the hills of central Tennessee, I was not meant to remain within the limits of that small world. As a good friend of mine put it so evocatively, I moved "from dirt to concrete." I was a bright-lights kinda' gal, someone who required the incitement of a more diverse, complicated way of life. I had to get out, and thus, I escaped north to the larger cities and taller buildings as soon as I was old enough to do so. I needed more: more stimulation, more opportunity, more intellectual and emotional challenges, more alignment between my inner and outer worlds. The slower, simpler South failed to satisfy me, and its naysaying culture failed to contain me. So, with an urgent yet hopeful heart, I went in search of an outside that matched my cramped yet determined insides.

One theory for my inevitable migration north is that I was switched at birth, perhaps through a mysterious armband swap in the hospital nursery. Or maybe I was a mishap in the gene pool, one of those oops-how-did-they-let-that-one-through? cases.

But a more likely theory is that without knowing it—and certainly never admitting it—my father raised me to be a feminist. He never once shied away from his belief–demonstrated in both word and action–that I could do whatever I set my mind to. His respect for both my academic and athletic prowess did not flinch. Even though I was a girl. A girl born in the South.

And so, I left my roots in search of a wider world, a world that could provide an oxygen mask for my restricted and slowly dying spirit. I went looking for an environment that would actively encourage my emotional, intellectual, and vocational wings to sprout.

Once gone, I did not look back. I never once seriously considered offers to "come home." And I received many such overtures. But the life I found and settled into north of the Mason-Dixon Line differs greatly from the one I was raised in. So different, in fact, that sometimes I don't even recognize the roots from which I came. My Northern world allows me to go on pretending that Tennessee is not in my blood.

That is, until I take a bite of crispy fried chicken or a fluffy warm biscuit. Or hear the sound of katydids at dusk on a summer evening or Johnny Cash's twang on a CD. Or smell the sweet scent of a magnolia blossom. Then, all of my senses conspire to cast me back to my Southern roots, leaving me lost and adrift on an unexpected wave of cultural and familial legacy.

Learning to "rough it" was an essential value in my rural childhood. Nature was the ultimate force to be reckoned with, and we Sullivans never backed down. Daring tenacity was part of our Sullivan inheritance, and being able to make do with less-than-ideal circumstances was deemed a high honor. We camped throughout the Great Smoky Mountains, pitching tents in the pouring rain. We hiked Mount Le Conte despite warnings of bear sightings. We flipped a canoe sideways over a twelve-foot-high waterfall on the Chattooga River—the same river where my father's all-time favorite movie, *Deliverance*, was filmed. We ran over rattlesnakes in the driveway and shot at innocent squirrels with BB guns in the backyard. My father and brothers hung deer antlers on the walls of our home as if they were expensive pieces of fine art. Something was not considered broken unless it could not be fixed with a roll of duct tape or a can of WD-40. It was like scenes out of a Southern reality television series, similar to the likes of *Duck Dynasty*.

When I got the bright idea of giving my kids a bit of Southern culture before they were lost to the metropolitan world of Washington, DC, my good-sport neighbor and friend, Patti, decided that she and her daughter would come along. Patti, being from urban Philadelphia, was not about to miss the chance for a little redneck adventure.

We set out for a twelve-mile canoe trip down the Shenandoah River; it was an excellent idea...or so I thought at first. The sun was cooperating. The water was bathwater warm. The coolers overflowed with enough junk food to last the entire outing. I was teaching my son how to steer a canoe and my daughter to get her feet dirty. Wouldn't dad be proud?

The kids were having a grand time. "Mom, can we do this every summer?" they yelled across the water, their words echoing through the riverbed canyons. I felt a moment of smug serenity; I was giving my kids a small taste of my Southern childhood, and they were delighted by it. They were enjoying being out in nature, away from their city lives.

However, after we stopped for our lunch of waterlogged PB&Js, I noticed a downshift in the mood. In her usual demure tone, Patti asked, "So how much longer do we have to go?"

Calmly, in a very what's-the-big-deal? Sullivanian way, I respond, "We're about halfway there."

Patti's face dropped like a boulder sinking to the bottom of the river. "You've got to be kidding me!" she politely muttered under her breath, both wanting and not wanting me to hear her complaint.

She sat there for a moment, stunned, silent, and frozen in place, clearly mulling over her options. You could smell her thoughts cooking. Should she turn around? Go forward? Stay there? Call a helicopter? Ride a cow? Hitchhike? Scream for help?

Finally, her voice resurfaced from the river's bottom. "Well... there's no going back. I've come this far; I guess I have no choice but to keep paddling."

And keep paddling she did. For six more long miles, my friend paddled one painful stroke after another, summoning strength she didn't know—or forgot—she had.

Now we can laugh about our big canoe adventure, even talk about how it represents life. We discuss how, once you get on the river, there is no stopping. It's like a moving walkway in an airport: a one-way journey that demands our commitment. We have no choice but to continue paddling, even when our body refuses to go on. We must dig deep within ourselves and pull one more stroke because we are not finished. We have yet to arrive at the endpoint, and there are six more miles remaining.

All the same, Patti made me promise that if we ever go again, we will sign up for a shorter canoe trip.

She may be right about this. Frequently, our lives require that we run plenty of long, excruciating marathons. A walk in the park might be a welcome relief. Besides, this Tennessee-born gal is still learning that not everything in life needs to be a hardship; not everything has to be held together with grit, duct tape, and a can of WD-40. Canoeing a short float down a river on a sunny day can be just as satisfying and worthwhile.

# 12

## *My Shabby Chic Dresser*

I admit it: I am–or am on the brink of becoming–a bargain addict. Whenever I find something cheap, my juices start flowing. "Ah-ha!" I think, fooling myself into believing that somehow, I have beaten the odds and discovered a rare, unlikely deal on a great item.

I must have inherited this trait from my father. He had a habit of bringing home random flotsam he noticed on the side of the road. Someone else's trash inevitably became his treasure. A worn-out broom, an industrial trash can, a broken chair, a used thingamabob—they all found a way into our home. Unwanted waste? Dad probably needed it. I can still hear my mother now: "Dickie, what is that? And why do we need it?" Despite her frustration, dad refused to give up his obsession of rummaging.

Like him, I'm always on the hunt for a good bargain. Whether it's cheap, free, or trash, I'm interested.

Then there was the case of the dresser. It "happened" across my laptop's screen one day—admittedly, while I was browsing eBay—as if to say, "Yours! Get it! You can't afford not to buy it!"

It was described as "chic and shabby," which sounded perfect–just my style. And at only twenty dollars, how could I go wrong? I excitedly dove to the next level of serious inquiry. With praiseworthy integrity, the seller warned me that one drawer was broken. Ha! As if that was going to stop me from pulling out my credit card. The seller had praised the dresser's charm, and at that price, I didn't think it could go awry. I was gleefully swimming in adrenal bathwater, already mentally making room for my new piece of furniture.

"When can you come pick it up? It's sitting in the garage, ready to go," the seller told me with a smug grin, one I could practically see through the phone, carried by the satisfaction in his voice at having found a sucker such as I.

Pick it up? I bristled at the unforeseen hurdle suddenly standing—looming, even—between my new chic and shabby acquisition and me. If I was remembering my geography correctly, Memphis, Tennessee, is quite a long drive from Washington, D.C.

My heart sank. But only momentarily. I had already emotionally committed to the damn thing. I wasn't about to give it up now. My mind raced, searching for a way to make this dream a reality.

"Can you ship it?" I replied.

"We can. We can get it to you via Greyhound for an additional $150." My heart plummeted into my stomach again, but my cognitive wheels refused to stop. Immediately, I justified this new expense. "That only makes my cheap dresser $170, right?" I asked myself. "That's still a good deal–even if one out of the three drawers is nonfunctional." I was fooling myself, by now an expert at creating lies even I would believe.

Also, since when was Greyhound in the delivery business? I had never heard of that, but then again, why not? The highways were full of stranger things. Either he was telling the truth, or I was a bargain-crazed fool. Either way, my now-multi-layered drama to get this broken, shabby dresser halfway across the country was still in play.

"Oh, I see," I demurred.

My mind kept going, refusing to let my budget-priced dresser go home with some else.

So let me get this straight in my own mind: I would have to rent a U-Haul truck to fetch my newest treasure from the bus station. That would be another fifty dollars–at least.

Chink, chink, chink.

And then, the crate with the busted, antiquated dresser would likely be so heavy I would have to beseech the bus driver to help me load it onto the truck. I'd then have to tip him for the years I had taken off his back.

Chink, chink, chink.

For the $250 I would now be spending on this broken castoff, I could have a brand-new dresser, one with no flaws or scratches, in perfect working order, and with all its drawers intact. On top of that,

I could even have it delivered directly to my house. But would it be "shabby and chic"? Of course not!

Or so I told myself.

"Sold!" I told the surprised and excited Memphian. I swear I could hear him sigh in relief. I'm sure he was just happy to gain more space in his garage.

So, a week later, after being carried by a Greyhound bus and a rented U-Haul truck, I finally got the $20-turned-$250 dresser into my house.

But that was only the beginning of the story.

My friend, whom I had begged to help me with this ridiculous two-person project of renting a truck, loading the dresser into said truck, and then unloading it again into my house, took one look at the now-unwrapped eyesore and asked in his most restrained tone, "What color do you plan on painting it?"

"Paint it?" I practically screamed. "I have no intention of painting it!" It was shabby and chic, one step short of falling apart, and I already was in love with it.

He ignored my vehement reaction, struggling to see what I saw in this piece of overpriced junk as he continued to inspect it. He eventually found enough generosity within himself to stretch beyond his taste buds and say placatingly, "Well, with a little of this and a little of that, I suppose it could be fixed up real nice."

"Now hold on right there!" I said, affronted. "You can't criticize my dresser. I got this great deal from Memphis, Tennessee. It traveled by bus all the way to my closet. It's old, Deco, half in pieces, and I already adore it just the way it is."

Despite my protests, after my friend left (not while he was still there—I was too full of pride), the first thing I did was find a hammer and some nails so as to fasten the broken drawer back together.

He was right—sort of. My dresser was *not* perfect the way it was. To most folks, it would be a twenty-dollar piece of shit, an object you give to Goodwill or sell on eBay to some trash-seeking, bargain-obsessed imbecile like me. But to me, my shabby chic dresser from the South was a prize that needed little rehabilitation to find its glory.

Perhaps it reminds me of me. I, like my newly acquired piece of falling-apart furniture, am showing a little wear and tear. The signs of my aging cannot be hidden–the wrinkles, the years, the mistakes, the regrets, the character imperfections, the cracks in my inner workings. I am far from flawless. I still have plenty of work to do to become who I want to be. *And* I want to be loved just the way I am. I am chic and shabby, yet I want to be accepted for who I am in this moment of my life, even if I too traveled a long road from Tennessee by way of many unpaved paths.

Maybe that's what we all long for: to be seen and loved for who we are today, while also being seen and loved for what we can be tomorrow.

I smile every time I look at my clunky dresser. My friend says he has come to like it the way it is. Granted, I need to be a little careful opening that fragile, piecemeal drawer, but our relationship had grown solid. We are in this for the long haul, and I wouldn't dare paint it now.

# 13
## *Kick His A\*\**

He needed another piece of me; one large piece was evidently not enough. He wanted not just more of my money, but also more of my time, more of my emotions, and most importantly, more of my children. Joint custody would not do anymore; he now required sole. He had to have it all. Sharing was never something he did well.

Three years had passed since our ugly divorce. I had settled into a different life with my part-time children. I bought a small, though expensive, shack north of Washington DC. We acquired a new full-time family member, a loud wrinkle-faced pug. The kids and I somehow made it work, and we had found a semblance of happiness—or at least as much as one can in a life we had never planned for or predicted.

When fresh, new, and different papers arrived via an innocent, underpaid courier on a frigid Friday evening during the early weeks of January 2012, I immediately realized the twelve months of the yet-to-be-filled calendar days had just been reserved. Just like that, my new year had been wrecked. Any hopes and dreams I had for that year had been stolen. Once again, I was the defendant, and if I did not oppose him, if I did not actively fight back, I would lose. And no mother I know would let her children go without a fight. Certainly not this one.

After a sleepless weekend of emotional shock and paralysis, the first call I made Monday morning was to my attorney. He was not surprised to hear from me, given his familiarity with my ex from the original go-around. My second phone call was to my psychiatrist. I would need medication to pull through a second act of this useless extended drama. He was not shocked to hear from me, either.

The weeks and months that followed unfolded painfully and tragically. The kids were inevitably and sadly sucked into the pointless, poisonous fight. They were old enough to have their own Guardian ad Litem, whatever the hell that is. She interviewed everyone, including them. During one of our private meetings, I sheepishly yet hopefully asked her if she knew anything about personality disorders. She looked dazed, as if she had no clue what I was referring to. I realized then that my trump card—my best chance at full and complete victory—was useless. My ex's charming personality would dazzle her, and the truth would remain obscured. Anyone can be a parent, and according to the law, every parent has the right to parent. Character is not deemed a deterrent.

My ex and I were both deposed by the respective opposing counsel. "Answer, 'Yes,' 'No,' or 'I don't recall,'" my attorney coached me. Six hours later, including a brief break to make a desperate last-minute call to my neighbor, asking her to pick up my kids from school, I had survived that hell. Little did I know it was only a warm-up for a soon-to-be greater hell, that of a full-blown custody trial.

As the weeks counted down to the proposed trial date, the last-minute legal theatrics quickened their pace. As I had already come to understand, the legal system thrives on crisis. The mounting pressure is intentional, as it generally forces one party to cave—a game of legal chicken.

A week before the proposed trial date, his legal team made me an unacceptable, ludicrous offer. I refused it. I was not giving up my children. Perhaps foolishly, I was convinced that they needed a mother, their mother.

Monday morning finally came. The trial was scheduled to begin at nine a.m. After getting my kids dressed, fed, and off to school, I showed up at the courthouse, trying to contain any unusual emotions on this most unusual of days. I outfitted myself thoughtfully and carefully: not too feminine, not too sexy, not too black, but a safe vanilla. As predicted, the judge delayed the trial, giving us extra time to "work this out." He sensed malarkey, accurately so.

But stubbornness prevailed. Extra time resolved nothing. Once again, a trial loomed.

As expected, my ex's charismatic charade and, likely, his money, had swayed the Guardian ad Litem. I was told that the judge would listen to her recommendation—one that slanted in my ex's favor. My attorneys and even my boyfriend had lost hope. They all advised me to fold, to take the so-called "joint custody" he was offering and give him what he wanted: all the time with and the decision-making power over my eleven-year-old son, whom I had adopted first, and my eight-year-old daughter, our biological child.

Every card was stacked against me: his money, his persuasive personality, the Guardian ad Litem's recommendation, and his high-powered, female-led attorney team. These factors all spoke to my demise in this contest. All I had on my side was my dogged belief that my children needed their mother. I refused to be swayed into believing my presence in their lives was not valuable.

Cornered and hopeless, I ended up sobbing in a windowless room outside our appointed courtroom. Time was ticking. My legal and emotional team seemed to have switched sides, leaving me alone at the most important crossroad of my life. My decision to either give in or go to trial would not only impact my life, but also—and more importantly—the lives of my young children who were depending on me. I was falling apart, frozen by the burden of responsibility and the likely dire outcome. In that moment, I was a full-fledged adult that desperately needed someone to take care of me. I was a parent in need of a parent.

I called the best substitute I had: my older brother. Rick and I had never been close while growing up; I had always connected more with my younger brother. But here, now, in this moment, it was Rick that I needed, and he showed up for me in spades.

Through a haze of tears and a mental fog, I explained my impossible dilemma: take what my ex offered and live with it, or go to trial and possibly lose more. To my surprise, I found myself saying, "Rick, what would dad tell me to do?" The words tumbled out of my mouth without my brain realizing what I had asked.

Before I could even finish the question, Rick emphatically gave his opinion: "He would tell you to go in there and kick his ass!" He assured me that my ex's "offer" was not joint custody—it was a face-saving version of golden handcuffs.

I knew he was right; it's exactly what dad would have advised.

With renewed energy, I returned to my lead attorney. "If we go to trial and I lose, what's the worst-case scenario?" I asked with a newfound calmness.

He explained that my ex could get sole legal and physical custody. I would see my children every other weekend…four days a month…48 of the 365 in a year. I took a deep breath and tried to wrap my brain around this horrific possibility—I knew there no way I could wrap my heart around it.

Then I turned back to my downcast lawyer, who no doubt felt he had failed me. "Well, if I'm going to get fucked," I said, "I'm at least going to get fucked by the judge. I want to go to trial."

Upon hearing my calmly decisive statement, my attorney did not hesitate. Within minutes, we were in the courtroom, ready to begin the three-day nightmare. Here I was, again, living life on the outskirts. Only 4 percent of custody cases actually go to trial, with only 1.5 percent completing custody litigation. I was about to be one of that 1.5 percent—not a statistic I wanted to boast about.

I settled into my seat, the one labeled, "Defendant." My heart steadied. I felt I had done the right thing. I would go down fighting.

After the first day of testimony, my case was undoubtedly going poorly. In fact, it was going horribly. My ex took the stand and said every imaginable–and unimaginable—nasty thing about me he could, accompanied by boxes and boxes of emails to "prove" I was unfit to be a mother to my own children. It was beyond bleak. Sleep would not have me that night.

As I drove back to the courthouse the next morning, mentally shoring up strength for another day, my cell phone rang. It was my legal team's second-in-command, begging me to give up. "Ginger, you need to fold and just sign his deal. As you know, yesterday didn't go well. You will lose."

But by now, warding off naysayers had become second nature. "I'm in now, and we will see this thing through," I told her before abruptly hanging up. I would not let her words penetrate my determination.

By the end of the second day, the tide had turned. Our character witnesses seemed to reflect our own characters: his was neutral and useless to his case, while mine was so helpful, my ex's attorney couldn't chase her off the stand fast enough. Our joint-parenting coordinator was evenhanded, speaking highly of us both. An email his legal team had intended to use to slight me was turned in my favor. During one glorious moment, the judge asked a witness of my ex, "Is he controlling?" I laughed to myself and kicked my attorney under the table, who tried to contain my enthusiasm by ignoring me.

The third day of the trial was all my attorney's show. The courtroom became his stage; my bilingual, junkyard dog of an attorney became the Alpha dog of the playground. A lawyer friend had recommended him years ago during the first go-around of my divorce. She had told me that he was cheap, but a top-notch litigator. And boy, was he. It was now his turn, and he ripped my ex and his overpriced legal team a new one. He was nothing less than brilliant.

But then, just as we prepared to open the champagne, in came that damned Guardian ad Litem who closed the trial by standing by her pre-trial recommendation. All our highs crashed. My heart plunged back to my feet.

The judge said he needed time to review the material and that he would be back within an hour with his verdict. I took a long walk around the courthouse in a vain attempt to maintain my sanity. I had no clue what my life would soon look like. What would I tell the kids if I lost? Would I pack up their belongings? How would I survive that new reality? Keeping my mind hopeful and calm proved to be impossible.

After what felt like an eternity, my attorney texted me to let me know the judge was back. "At least," I told myself, "this hell will be over."

The judge began his decision with sarcastic congratulations, stating that we had just wasted a lot of time and money slinging mud at each other. He said, in his position, he had seen truly "bad" parents over the years, and neither of us were they. He declared that not only was he leaving the custody arrangement as-is, with joint legal and physical custody, but he was giving me more time with our children.

We won. (Not that anyone ever really does in these horrid situations.) Standing up for my children and being victorious—despite my underdog status—was no small feat. We were David with his useless slingshot, taking down fancy-pants Goliath.

The date was September 26, the exact day my father had been killed in a hunting accident twenty-five years earlier. Perhaps it was sheer coincidence, but September 26 now needed to take on additional meaning and significance.

As we walked out of the courthouse that afternoon, my attorney was dumbfounded. Now that the trial was over, he could share his opinions with me honestly. He never thought we could win. He confessed that this had been one of the two most difficult trials of his career. We had just sunk the Titanic. He told me to go home, hug my kids, have a glass of wine, and get ready for another round, because my ex would certainly come after me again.

It seems absurd to say that one of the signature moments of my life was also one of the most painful, but it's true. I have no idea where the grit and resilience came from to counter not only my ex and his legal team, but also to stand up to my team of advisors, to keep going when almost everyone was telling me to give up.

I guess we never really know our own strength until we have no choice but to reach in and find it. When we need it most, it appears out of nowhere. Like a lifesaving piece of wood that bobs up in a rocking ocean, we grab hold of it and hang on. Something inside arises from seemingly nothing.

Today, my almost-grown kids and I are settled comfortably. Life in our overpriced shack with our smoosh-faced pug continues. My children are living as they ought: with a relationship with both of their parents, two people that are neither all good nor all bad. We're both just flawed human beings making an imperfect go of it. Such is all any of us can ever do.

# 14
## *Pulling Teeth*

No one had ever dared attempt it before, at least within the male gender. Breaking family tradition can be risky.

You see, I come from a long line of dentists. And I mean *very* long. Both of my grandfathers were dentists. Additionally, my maternal grandfather was a professor at a dental school. My father was a dentist and was slated to be the next President of the Tennessee Dental Association before his untimely death. His only brother, my uncle, is a dentist. Both of my brothers are dentists. My cousin is a dentist. So is my second cousin. My nephew just completed dental school and joined my brother's practice, which had been my father's practice. And, predictably, my parents met at a dental convention. Is it merely by chance that all these men—and notice, they are all men—have a passion for teeth, or is it a sign of family dysfunction?

To his non-gender-biased credit, my father encouraged me to join the family vocation and become a dentist. I too could have pursued the familial occupation and become the first female in the family to possess the title Doctor of Dentistry. I, however, gladly passed up the opportunity. It was clear from a young age that my chosen path did not wind through other peoples' mouths.

Before I was of legal working age, I was assisting my dad in his dental office during the summer months. I think my official title was "Go-'Fer," as in, "Go get this," or "Go bring me that." I spent much of my time washing and sterilizing the bloody dental instruments, then carefully following the color-coded pictures to organize the trays for upcoming patients. I even figured out which procedure required which type of tray: yellow for checkups, orange for cavities, and green for surgeries—those last types were the procedures that called for the scary-looking tools. I restocked supplies and did all the other distasteful grunt work nobody else wanted to do.

Spending my summers in the bowels of a dental office gave me enough of a firsthand view into the day-to-day life in the teeth profession to know it wasn't for me. Don't get me wrong; as a preteen, I loved the paycheck. Seven dollars an hour felt like abundant riches. And the flexible hours the boss allowed? Plus the ability to just take off for the movies any afternoon I wanted? It was summer-job perfection. But putting my hands in peoples' mouths all day long for thirty years? Trying to make one-way small talk while the other party is gagging? Having to tolerate the sight of blood? Causing all that pain? Having people hate you because they fear you? Nope, not for me. I never even considered it as a professional option.

Besides, with all those dentists, I figured the family needed a good shrink. The rest is history. I am the lone ranger, the only one to carve an uncharted vocational path within my family.

Still, what has surprised me as my psychotherapy career has unfolded is that perhaps I chose the family business after all.

Just like with a dentist, folks come to me in pain and want me to "fix" them. And, not only do they want me to "fix" them, but they also want a cure that is instantaneous and pain-free.

Like a dentist, I too am frequently feared and hated. To heal a wound, I must often dig under and around it, which can temporarily cause more pain. The rawness of the unfamiliar is often excruciating. But unlike in dentistry, I cannot offer a shot of anesthesia or a dose of laughing gas to ease the process. Sometimes, it just hurts like hell.

Like a dentist, I teach preventative care. Instead of brushing and flossing, I teach emotional literacy and relational effectiveness. My job is to help a patient fire me. When my work is complete, my counsel is no longer necessary.

And like a dentist, I extract many teeth. Folks come to my office and insist they want help; something in their life is not working. Most of the time, patients claim something or someone outside of themselves is the problem. The finger-pointing begins; if I could simply change their spouse or boss, they'll be happy. Of course, it's often something within them that needs alteration, not those around them. The long, slow process of getting someone to see this is like pulling teeth. In psychotherapy, we call it resistance.

As we begin the process of uncovering what needs to shift and why it has not changed before, we often hit Newton's third law: every action has an equal and opposite reaction. If I push one way, the patient will undoubtedly pull the other way.

"You mean you want me to do that?" retorts the patient.

"You mean you want me to adjust that?" he or she complains.

Heels dig in. Walls like Fort Knox's solidify. Self-protection becomes the patient's primary motivation, and his or her defenses become almost impossible to penetrate. The roots of that tooth seem permanently imbedded.

Dr. Suess was familiar with this dilemma. He explained it perfectly in melodic rhyming poetry in his classic children's book, *Green Eggs and Ham*. As a refresher for anyone who hasn't read it in awhile, this annoying little varmint tries to persuade an older, wiser creature that if only he would try green eggs and ham, he would love them. The more the seller tries to convince his potential customer that he really will appreciate this unsightly meal, the more the older guy runs for the hills in resistance. But the seller is persistent. He skitters optimistically from a boat to a moat to a goat, trying to sway his target he has something he will enjoy, something he even needs. And out of perhaps sheer exhaustion or at least the hope of finally getting rid of this pest, the old guy surrenders. He tastes the goods, and the tide turns.

"Thank you, thank you, Sam-I-am. I do so like green eggs and ham."

Like the annoying Sam-I-Am, I too must seduce patients into accepting what I have to share. But once they decide to receive my offering, they usually end up leaving with more than they had initially come to me seeking—often something they didn't even know they needed.

But unlike the patients that sit in the dental chairs of my kinfolk, my patients are not passive objects who are knocked out, drugged-up, and unable to talk back. Would that it were so. In that way, dentistry seems almost like cheating…you lie there sedated and let the doctor do all the work. Not so in my office. Cooperation is required, and the process, often challenging. Yes, I too relieve the pain that brought patients to my office in the first place; I heal the hurts they carry unnecessarily and, likely, unknowingly. But I do not simply stop there. I want to make them better than ever, better than they even knew they could be.

If you run into any male Dr. Sullivans from the South, chances are, he's a dentist. And if he is a dentist, chances are he's a relative of mine. That being said, I too carry on the family tradition by pulling teeth in my neck of the woods, in a way I prefer to do it: by removing character traits and behaviors that are no longer useful and are causing more pain than help, by teaching effective tools to get the emotional nourishment one needs, by sharpening a better bite for when life demands that one take care of one's self, and by polishing a healthy smile to flash should a moment of joy be uncontainable.

# 15

## *The Center Hill Hyatt*

As we pulled onto the salvage lot's gravel drive, an older-looking man came out of his makeshift office on wheels. His cavalier grin gave the impression he didn't care whether he made a sale that day; he was content either way.

"May I help yous?" he asked in his long, slow Southern drawl, not looking up to see who or what had pulled onto his property. This strange old man spooked us kids, so we hunkered down behind our white vintage truck as my father braved the words, "We've come to buy a trailer. You got one for sale?"

"I reckon I do," the man mumbled under his breath, subtly motioning for us to follow him. He clearly did not want to put any more energy into his day than he absolutely had to.

Like an absent-minded flock, we followed the strange man's orders. For some reason, we were entrusting this half-alive man with materializing our dream country home. Dad's choices had such power over us.

"Over yonder. That's what we got," he said after a short walk, pointing to what looked like a few dilapidated structures. There weren't many options, and, to me, they all appeared the same: small, white, tasteless, and classless. After a round of family eeny-meeny-miny-moe, we selected our prized second home.

In some ways, I suppose you could say I was reared in a trailer. Or at least I was during the summers. That trailer was part of the landscape of my childhood; it was our lakeside abode on Center Hill Lake in the hills of central Tennessee.

When I was fourteen years old, my dad finally decided to do something with a small plot of land he owned, which had remained unbeknownst to me until that point. It was an acre of unspoiled lakeside property he had purchased at the age of nineteen. He and some fishing buddies had resolved that they needed to each own a piece of the property they so loved. They had the foresight and the wherewithal to scrape together enough of their side-job money to buy in early. Thus, they bought into paradise, their paradise, a sliver of their teenage playground.

The first stop in this unfolding family dream was the trailer sales lot. What looked like a scrapyard on the "other side" of town held the contraption that would make up the next chapter in our family story. Yes, we had to buy one of those God-awful, plastic, molded, prefabricated, cookie-cutter homes on wheels. To put on the lakefront acreage, the piece of heaven from my dad's boyhood.

Getting this unsightly monstrosity to its new home would not be a simple matter. Halfway down the hill to the chosen spot, the truck towing the trailer got stuck in thick Tennessee mud. Neither the truck nor the trailer would budge.

"Didn't I see a farm up the road with a large John Deere tractor?" my dad asked no one in particular, engaging his resourceful duct-tape-and-WD-40 mentality of "We can fix anything." Before any of us could respond, we were headed back up the gravel road to the unknown farmer with the big green tractor. We were complete strangers asking to borrow a multi-thousand-dollar investment. None of us even imagined that the farmer would say no.

The stranger's John Deere tractor did get our new trailer home unstuck and nestled safely in its hillside spot, overlooking the pristine Center Hill Lake of Smithville, Tennessee.

This white trailer became our second home. It was part of my dad's secret strategy to keep the teenagers close and under his watchful eyes. Create a fun atmosphere of waterskiing, summer sun, and food and not only would the teenagers stick around, but their friends would join in. No need to worry about where and with whom the kids were. If you build it, they will come.

His plan worked, too. Every summer weekend, family and friends gathered at our trailer home—the Center Hill Hyatt, as we sarcastically dubbed it. It was ninety minutes from the hustle and bustle of our regular daily lives, a home-away-from-home where life took on a different meaning and moved at a slower pace. Not only was it less stressful, it was also, shall we say, crude. Our trailer had no running water or indoor plumbing—just a tin roof, a mouse-infested floor, and fifty feet of barely cleared path to the outdoor privy. Mind you, one with a glorious view. I bet you've never pooped amidst such beauty.

Sounds hideous, I know. But it truly was bliss. It was water mixed with sunshine. A relaxed father in a good mood. Learning to slalom on calm, glasslike, warm water. Devouring chess cake and homemade chocolate chip cookies from 1970s Tupperware that held their freshness. Sporting a Hawaiian Tropic tan long before skin cancer was a concern. Sleeping on a screened-in porch and listening to unknown noises coming from the surrounding forest. What's not to love about all that?

And then there were additional adventures, like learning to drive without a formal lesson.

"We're out of water!" mom would often yell from the trailer's kitchen.

"I'll go!" we three kids always screamed in unison, fighting over the car keys, the ultimate driver's age being irrelevant.

Children driving. Without a license. Barely able to see over the dashboard. Up the gravel road a mile to the more civilized neighbor with the red brick house, who kindly allowed us to use their outdoor spigot to fill former plastic milk jugs with water, so mom could wash the breakfast dishes. Yes, I was reared in the South.

Our Center Hill lake house was the family's haven, so much so that my brothers have maintained the tradition. Mind you, they've upgraded from the trailer. They both own second lake homes that outclass my first home. My Northern kids love to visit.

"Mom, can we move to Tennessee?" they ask every time we must say goodbye to the mixture of lake water and family fun. Each time they ask, I cringe. My insides twist in tumult. I laugh while internally crying. Can they not appreciate the different life I carved out for them all on my own? The one that gives them a wider geographical, intellectual, and cultural field on which to play and explore?

Do they want to take this train backwards when I have worked so hard to progress it forward?

Then, I calm myself. They don't understand because they can't. They only know what they have been exposed to. Once the light has been turned on, we can't turn it off again. At least for now, my children must live where I choose to.

My older brother, Rick, once told me something quite telling long ago when his children were young. He innocently and sweetly stated that he would travel with his kids. He would take them far and wide, expand the horizon whence our parents had travelled with us. "I will take my kids to Alabama, Mississippi, South Carolina, North Carolina, and Georgia!" he proudly proclaimed.

I tried not to burst out laughing. I didn't have the heart to point out that those locales are all still in the South, that he could take them to California, Chicago, Paris, Rome, Seattle–just to name a few wider-world options. But rather than pointing out the obvious, at least to me, I nodded and smiled, loving him for who he is while being reminded, yet again, of how different I am.

Last year, my niece chose Center Hill as the location for her wedding. It was a combination of Jane Austen and country elegance, a vision she had cherished for as long as she could play princess. I was happy that her dreams were manifesting exactly as she imagined they would.

The morning of her nuptials, it poured rain. As she primped her hair and nails—those final details in anticipation of her future—I was cast backwards, reflecting on what was and what will never be again. My niece grows up; I grow young. She progresses; I regress. Old submerged emotions of loss, pain, and disconnection from my childhood resurfaced without my permission. Feelings are so damn renewable that way.

"Hello," they said. "It's me again." As if I wouldn't recognize them.

The young girl inside me, the one buried under this aging face and sagging body, had returned. For the umpteenth time, I was given the opportunity to circle back around and pick up more pieces of myself. This time, it was the parts of me that spent many a weekend at Center Hill Lake basking in the sun, arguing with my parents, deciding if I should have another cookie or not and how far I would go with my boyfriend that night.

Thankfully, on this forced jaunt into my unfledged inner self, I could marshal more tenderness, curiosity, and kindness than usual. I could agree that my kids are right–Tennessee is not such a bad place. Not that I am ever moving back. But, it's a great place to be… from. I originated within these hollows, and there are still gifts for me to find in the rolling green hills of central Tennessee.

It did eventually stop raining that night. The evening of my niece's promise to love forever, the moon turned up and shone through the leftover clouds, casting a sparkling shadow on the pristine lake of Center Hill. I took an extra minute to pause and notice it while the others rushed to the dance floor. I gladly acknowledged that young girl deep within me. Undeniably, her roots run Southern. My heart was at peace.

# 16
## *Loving the Life You Have*

I swear it happens weekly: I open my mouth, and some store clerk or new patient or person on the street asks me where I'm from. I feel like a transplant from a foreign land. Even though I left decades ago and have successfully eradicated the "y'all"s and the "yonder"s from my vernacular, my Southern upbringing still comes through loud and clear in my slight, yet permanent, twang.

Alas, my migration north did not erase my history. Although I may try to disguise my background, I know it's impossible. My roots will not, cannot, be denied.

Here in the North, for reasons both obvious and not-so-obvious, the South is not looked upon too kindly. There exists a posture of looking down one's nose at those south of the Mason-Dixon Line. My accent alone can often lead to questions, possibly even judgments, which leave me squatting in shame through no fault of my own. I can practically hear their thoughts: "Is she as stupid as she sounds?" "Did she grow up in a trailer park?" "Is she small-minded, racist, conservative, and overly religious?"

I feel like I'm constantly trying to prove myself worthy. It's exhausting. And ridiculous. "Don't write me off!" my insides shriek. "See me! Look past my inflection. Give me a chance. I can hang with you Yankee intellectuals. I am worldly. I am not a mindless Southern belle. I can contribute something of value. *I am good enough.*"

Growing up Southern is my narrative, and there is not a damn thing I can do about it.

But stereotypes stand for a reason. And many of them are true.

Yes, there were guns in my house. Several, in fact. My brother once shot a hole in the floor by accident while on his way to kill a squirrel in the backyard—his form of afternoon amusement.

Yes, we ate our share of greasy fried chicken and cheesy, buttery grits. One grandmother made amazing homemade biscuits I still cannot duplicate. The other grandmother set a mean formal dining table and needed three black helpers–a gardener, a cook, and a housekeeper–to maintain her immaculate world.

Yes, my brother's sixth-grade science fair project comprised a full-sized reconstructed cow skeleton, which he had unearthed from the field across the street. It won first place. You cannot make this shit up.

Yes, our family said grace before meals and dressed for church every Sunday.

Yes, the daily beverage of choice was sweet iced tea, even for youngsters.

Yes, we spent our weekends canoeing or watching SEC football—our second religion.

Furthermore, no woman in our family worked outside the home. We were marriage material only, groomed to be fine window dressing, rather than intellectual or financial equals.

My heart was the first to notice I was suffocating. It was death by disconnection. I wanted a vaster world, one that talked to me, stimulated me, expanded me. From a young age, I felt alone, and I did not have the words or the ability to identify my predicament, much less fix it. I was surrounded by superficial nicety and put-together beauty, while my soul longed for authenticity. I could not pretend, and my attempts at trying were slowly killing me. I assumed that something must be wrong with me. After all, why was everyone else around me happily masquerading, while I was nauseous and undernourished?

And then there was my intellect. Southern girls were not supposed to be smart and use their intelligence; we were meant to get married young, have babies, and stay married forever, comfortably relying on our husbands to take care of us. To my parents' credit, they educated me well, sending me to the best private schools available. I'm sure that, originally, the Harpeth Hall School was a finishing school for Southern ladies. But even the South could not stay in the dark forever, keeping bright young female minds contained. At some point, and certainly gradually, the all-girls school instead became a launching pad for well-to-do families to provide their daughters with opportunity. I'm grateful my parents had such foresight.

But even there, I was more backwoods than most. I didn't fit into the prep-school world.

I will never forget the middle school quiz bowl. The announcer read off vocabulary words to the competing panelists. The girls on stage, all smarter than me, reeled off the definitions one by one. I had never even heard some of the terms before.

Suddenly, the announcer called out, "Taxidermist. T-A-X-I-D-E-R-M-I-S-T. Taxidermist."

The room fell silent. Every smart girl on stage was stumped. No one knew what that word meant.

The announcer then turned to the audience and asked if anyone there knew the correct definition of the word.

I knew what "taxidermist" meant. Hell, we had a few on the family payroll that occasionally came to Sunday dinner. I slowly raised my shy hand and gave the correct answer. More than a few stares shot my way. "Who is *that* girl?" likely crossed several minds.

Fast-forward multiple decades. I have not lived south of the Mason-Dixon Line for a long time. But whenever I have a chance to visit, a part of me, deep down in my DNA, awakens and says "home." Maybe it's the sound of the katydids or the fragrant smell of freshly cut green grass. Whatever the trigger, my emotions of yesteryear, feelings attached to the place of my upbringing, rise with intensity and demand my sentimental attention.

When folks in my everyday life hear that I am from Tennessee, they cannot camouflage their reactions—some mix of mockery, ridicule, and disbelief. When they think of the state of my origin, they likely imagine overweight stupid people that talk funny, pray to Jesus, and vote for Donald Trump. That mental image is mostly accurate. But all the same, hailing from Southern soil is my story. I am all of what I have come from.

Over the years, I have managed to willingly—even proudly—claim a part of my Southern heritage. The art of setting an elegant table is important, as is the act of taking a home-cooked meal to a fallen-ill neighbor. There is something dignified in my child's "Yes, ma'am," and "No, sir," that just sounds better than a bare "Yeah." I understand that dressing up a statement to make it seem kinder goes a lot farther than naked aggression. Thus, I have resolved that perhaps my Southern line wasn't all bad. Maybe there are parts of my upbringing I can redeem and even hold on to.

Undeniably, whether I appreciate it or not, being reared in the South is my story. I often say, "I'm not sure I like the path I took to get here, but I like the me I am now." And I would certainly not be the me I am now without having spent eighteen years wading barefoot in the creek and watching my dad chase loose cows down the street.

Our lives are like a blank twelve-foot-by-twelve-foot wall, just waiting to be filled with our individual murals. The totality of our experiences is painted there. We can try to draw over or around parts or make them into something else, but nothing is erasable. We are the sum of all our encounters throughout our lives.

However, the good news is that our artwork is not complete until our journey ends. We can always add more to our masterpiece, which can transform the composition's entirety. We are a continuous work-in-progress.

I don't know about you, but that works for me. It generates hope. It fortifies self-compassion. On a good day, it allows me to embrace the life I have now.

I am reminded of that old Crosby, Stills, and Nash song, "Love the One You're With." I may not have the life I wanted, the life I dreamt of, but I am learning to love the life I have.

So pass the biscuits and pour the iced tea. I'm gonna treat myself to all of it. Every last bite.

# Acknowledgements

Nothing happens in isolation. There are invariably cheers from an expectant crowd, cries that occur before there is even anything to cheer. External noise requires delivery. To that, I am beholden.

Thank you to my college professors, Dr. Rich Butman and Joan Stough, who discovered I had something to say underneath my shy demeanor.

Thank you to Elliot, my psychoanalyst, who is the keeper of my story. Eighteen years ago, in a chance group session at the American Group Psychotherapy Association, he ordered me, "Open your god-damn mouth." I've been recovering my words ever since.

Thank you to David Allen, Nancy Reid, George Shapiro, Laura Young, Patti Hoath, Cherie Morris, Elizabeth Barrett, Erik Kispert, Jane Beresforde, and Mark Wadley, who summoned me to continue writing.

Thank you to my dear friend, Jennifer Boykin. Having wanted to write a book forever, I was leaning toward self-help. Over flavorless Denny's, she demanded that I put my essays out into the world first. She is always right.

Thank you to Kathryn Johnson, my extreme writing coach. You were there at the finish to help push the baby out.

Thank you to my editor, Elisabeth Chretien. You took a chance on me as a new writer. I appreciate your voice of reason peppered with some much-needed encouragement.

Thank you to Beth Leoni for the fabulous cover design. You make the book's insides shine from the outside. I appreciate your capturing the spirit of my words and amplifying it. (Beth can be found at JBCL2006@yahoo.com.)

Thank you to my mother, who came to appreciate my off-beaten path and found love for the daughter she did not intend to have. You expanded your comfort zone, and I am thankful for your support.

Thank you to my brothers who lived through many of these stories alongside me. We are often too proud to say it aloud, but I know we have each other's backs. Come visit some time. I promise you'll return to the South untainted.

Thank you to Jen Pastiloff for publishing my first essay. While I was crying at the kitchen table as my inaugural launch into the digital world was underway, this unknown woman kept sending me encouraging texts.

Thank you to Carlos Salvado and Soon Ei Sweeney, my underdog attorneys. Never say "never," especially to a Southern gal.

Thank you to my patients, my students, and my blog and Facebook page readers. I have not met and likely will never meet many of you, yet every now and again, you mention that my work and words make a difference. You are the lifeline that keeps me typing.

And I am indebted to my family: Aidan, Isabel, and my fiancé, Joe. You are the real-life human beings with whom I rub elbows every day, the ones who see the Wizardess behind the curtain. Thank you for tolerating all my shushing, my early morning writing hours, and my many absences so that my internal voice could find its words. Without you, dreams would remain just that—dreams. I love you more.

# *Disclaimer*

All the events portrayed in this book are based on my own recollections, and I recognize that others may remember things differently. I have related my impressions to the best of my ability without the intent to harm. Some identities have been altered or are composites.

**Ginger M. Sullivan, MA, LPC, CGP, FAGPA**, *is a practicing psychotherapist in Washington DC. She writes about the human experience–life's raw, real underbelly–so that others might continue their own journeys to become their highest, best selves. She lives in Montgomery County, Maryland, with her fiancé, two children, and one grouchy pug. To get a daily dose of her random musings, you can find her at*
www.facebook.com/gingersullivanpc/ *or*
www.gingersullivan.org.

CPSIA information can be obtained
at www.ICGtesting.com
Printed in the USA
BVHW03*0913040818
523228BV00001B/2/P